TRACING IT HOME

LYNN PAN

TRACING IT HOME

A Chinese Family's Journey from Shanghai

KODANSHA INTERNATIONAL
New York • Tokyo • London

Kodansha America, Inc.,
114 Fifth Avenue, New York, NY 10011, U.S.A.

Kodansha International, Ltd.,
17-14 Otowa 1-chome, Bunkyo-ku, Tokyo 112, Japan

First published in the United States in 1993 as *Tracing It Home:
A Chinese Journey* by Kodansha America, Inc.
Originally published in Great Britain in 1992 as *Tracing It
Home: Journeys Around a Chinese Family*
by Martin Secker & Warburg Limited.

The lines on p. v are from "Continuing to Live,"
in *Collected Poems* by Philip Larkin, and are quoted
by permission of Farrar, Straus & Giroux.
The extract on p. 37 is from the essay *The Ningpo* Pang *and
Financial Power at Shanghai* by Susan Mann Jones
in *The Chinese City Between Two Worlds,* edited by Mark Elvin
and G. William Skinner, reproduced by kind permission of
Stanford University Press.

Library of Congress Cataloging-in-Publication Data

Pan, Lynn.
Tracing it home : a Chinese family's journey from Shanghai /
Lynn Pan.
p.   cm.
ISBN 1-56836-043-6
1. Pan, Lynn—Journeys—China—Shanghai.   2. Authors
English—20th century—Biography.   3. Shanghai (China)—
Description and travel.   I. Title.
PR6066.A47T73   1993
951'.132—dc20   93-20563

Printed in the United States of America

95 96 97 98 99 Q/FF 10 9 8 7 6 5 4 3 2 1

... in time,
We half-identify the blind impress
All our behavings bear, may trace it home.

Philip Larkin

Author's Note

Purists will, I hope, forgive me my mixing of Pinyin romanization with older conventions: it is impossible to be entirely consistent and at the same time to escape pedantry. To spare people's feelings, I have changed a few names.

It is a pleasure to record my gratitude to the two people who, through their hospitality in Shanghai and London, helped me in the writing of this book: Tess Johnston and Catherine Stenzl. I am equally grateful to Margaret Scott and Jonathan Friedland, who read and gave me their thoughts on the manuscript.

London and Hong Kong, 1991

1

This is the family grave. Inside these English hedges, in this corner of a north London cemetery, I stand on the spot where my father meant us all to be buried – himself, his wife, his daughter and his son. Before me is the tombstone, a little stained by bird droppings; behind me a tall pine, the classical symbol of constancy and longevity. The stone, high and grey, is a polished slab of granite from Scotland. The epitaph was wrought by an English craftsman, tracing the Chinese characters from a sheet of rice paper which my father had commissioned a well-known calligrapher in Taiwan to inscribe.

Here I linger, as I often do, and because the lunar calendar tells me it is the Pure Brightness Festival, the Chinese All Souls' Day, a day traditionally marked by commemorations and supplications before the family grave. In Chinese cemeteries all over the world, men, women and children will be arriving with incense and dishes of cooked food, to wish the spirits well and maybe to have a picnic in the graveyard.

But here I am alone, and instead of food offerings I lay a bunch of daffodils. The sun, after rain, touches the damp grass at my feet. Winter is lasting into spring in a rawness in the air. I stand before the memorial, reading the two sets of names, of person and native place; and the dates, of birth and death. The years are connected by a small engraved hyphen representing life; and seeing it I think, Neither of my parents was of an age to die.

I think of my father, and how he came to choose England for the family grave. Exiled like millions of other Chinese by the communist revolution in China, my father was then living in Malaysia; he could, I suppose, have chosen to site his grave there. Malaysia had certainly been good to him: it had allowed him to prosper. His connections with England, on the other hand, were tenuous, to say the least. It is true that I was living here, but if he felt like seeing me he would just as soon arrange to meet me elsewhere, in the course of either his travels or mine. No, apart from his liking for British gaming laws and the roulette wheels at the Ritz Club, he had no particular reason to think well of this country.

One thing had simply led to another. A few months before I was due to take my finals at Cambridge, where I was reading for a degree, I learned that my mother was suffering from aplastic anaemia, and that she would die within a year. She was in California at the time, consulting a specialist at the Stanford Medical School, and I had heard the doctor's verdict when I'd phoned her from Cambridge. This American specialist had said that there was nothing he could do for her, and it would be best if she were to spend the coming months at a place where she could have her family about her, and where, at the same time, she could receive better medical care than in Malaysia. On learning she had a daughter living in London, he had considered it a good idea for her to come here immediately, and had referred her to a haematologist he knew at the Hammersmith Hospital.

I went to meet her at Heathrow Airport. She was a terrible colour, surviving on blood transfusions, but no one over whom death hovered could be calmer or more matter-of-fact. What lay before her was an unknown ordeal, a helplessness not the less terrible for being unacknowledged. But we greeted each other impassively, even formally. We were not Latins, after all; no physical demonstration of emotion seemed permissible, no hugging, no grasping of hands. Just as calmly we drove into central London, where my father took a flat; and there she settled in quietly, joined a little later by my brother from Malaysia.

When the end came, only three months after her prognosis was confirmed, it was much sooner than any of us had expected. It was as if she had told herself, Better get it over with; my mother had always hated to put people to too much trouble. Her life had been signally without equivocation, and it was we who dithered, faced suddenly with the question of what arrangements to make for her funeral. The question would not have arisen if we had still been living in the old China, where the family grave would be awaiting recruits to join the fathers, mothers, the grandparents and the great-grandparents. But she had died in a foreign country; here decisions would not be lifted out of our hands by immemorial practice.

Were her ashes, boxed in a bronze chest, to be interred in England; or was my father to take them back with him? It was back at the flat, in the small hours of the morning my mother died, that we pondered this question. That there had to be a tomb was never in any doubt. 'But a plot,' said my father; 'we'd have to buy a plot somewhere.' The Chinese ideal would be some spot in one's native town or village, where the grave could be frequently visited by one's descendants; in Chinese the word for 'death' is an ideograph showing a figure kneeling before his ancestors' bones.

My father could not imagine the mechanics of the arrangements, in a country so unfamiliar to him, but he was convinced of

3

their necessity, and more than a little concerned that I should not, on their account, miss my exams in Cambridge. These were starting the next day, advanced by two weeks so as not to clash with the Queen's Jubilee celebrations. He said, as if solving a problem for both of us, 'If your mother hadn't wanted you to take your degree she wouldn't have died when she did.'

I did not know how to talk to him, about this or any other subject. Up till now, any approach to him would have been made through the intermediary of my mother; he was the traditional father, distant and feared, coming late to the emotional side of parenthood, the side of which my mother had assumed almost the entire part.

A silence fell between us, and some long minutes dragged by. Then my father, never a character to be at a loss for long, brightened visibly, as he formed at last the unprompted idea.

'Harrods,' he announced.

To find his plot, he would seek the services of Harrods, the place where, as I believe the saying goes, you can get anything from a pin to an elephant.

So Harrods it was. The funeral department there came to his aid, offering a choice of sites like any estate agent. Everything thereafter took place without a hitch; I left, lulled by Valium, to sit my finals at Cambridge; in London a plot in a well-tended cemetery was applied for and granted.

'Just the thing,' my father said to me when I returned to London; he already sounded as if his anguish was a long way behind. The plot, in the shape of a triangle, had room for nine graves, and standing on the path to its left you had a view of hills, their blue whitened by distance. A fresh posy lay on a neighbouring grave. Chestnut trees, their leaves thickening with the season, added to the Englishness of the scene.

I could tell my father was pleased with this spot, though he saw it with different eyes from mine; to him what counted was the siting of the grave, which he pronounced to be of good *fengshui*, using the Chinese term for 'geomancy', literally meaning 'winds and waters'. I was glad that he thought so, because people of his generation are still held by the ancient idea that if the tombs of the dead were not properly positioned, evil effects would befall the descendants of those whose bodies lay in them; conversely, good siting could conduce to their health, wealth and happiness.

The bright surface of my father's modernity hid a mixture of superstition and conventionality. The night my mother died, after two days in coma, he was at a casino in the West End, trying to dispel for a little while the agony of having watched her for hours at the hospital. When my brother phoned from the hospital, and he heard his name called over the intercom system, at that moment the roulette wheel came to rest at a number. 'I knew then that that was the end,' he later told me, 'because the number at which the wheel stopped was zero.' I relate this not very significant event to illustrate the fact that however often he made judgements of reason, upon his deepest beliefs they had no effect.

As if to quell any lingering misgivings in himself, he said to me, looking at the grave, 'It's good that we settled on England; it is a country which has been as stable as any for the longest time.' China with its revolutions was in both our minds. It always amazes me to hear an English friend say, of an ornament or a plate or a ring, 'It was my grandmother's' – suggesting a continuity to life quite inconceivable to me. I am never more struck by this continuity than when I glimpse those old women who prise apart lace curtains and gaze from rooms where they have slept all their lives and will die.

It was a sunless morning, dead still. Gazing at the unweeded plots which faced us wherever we turned, my father observed, disapprovingly, 'Few of these graves can have been visited by the families.' He lit a cigarette as we turned our steps towards the car, and he seemed as much alone as if I hadn't been there. But a little later he spoke again, and what he said startled me; he said, with what I felt to be immense remoteness, 'Your grandfather's grave has been dug up. More than once.'

I wanted to ask, Why? When? Was it the communists? But as I stole a glance at his face his remoteness checked me, and it struck me with something of a shock that he had never spoken of his father so spontaneously before. I knew he had far more to say if he could but find the means, and I realized all at once that as a child he had had to conceal his innermost feelings. That habit he had maintained throughout life; and now he was incapable of breaking down the barriers which he had put up between himself and certain areas of his early life.

There was much that I, for my part, wanted to say. I wanted to ask him about his family, and the past in which, for some reason, he seemed to take no interest. But we had never talked of things so intimate as that; there are questions which if not asked at the start are not asked later. What I knew of his family I had largely learned from my mother, and that was little enough. By the time I was of an age to be curious about such matters I was no longer living in the same country, and my parents and I seldom saw each other. Now I felt indescribably bereaved, a mourner over an unrecoverable past.

2

There was still an hour to go before the rites began. I sat in the main hall of the monastery, not knowing what to expect. Long ago and almost at random, it seemed, inscriptions had been painted on walls and pillars. Idly I read the words, THE SEA OF PAIN HAS NO BOUNDS; REPENT AND BE SAVED. The word 'Rulai', Chinese for Tathagata, a title of the Buddha meaning 'He who has thus come', caught my eye; I repeated it to myself, to have something to do.

My father and brother sat in a row on my right; my mother's sister Ming and her maid Ah Sam on my left. As the only true Buddhist amongst us, Ah Sam was the one who had made all the arrangements with the monastery for masses for my mother's soul to be performed. She had said to my father that really, he mustn't content himself with just a 'foreign-style' memorial service in England, and he had repaid her concern by appointing her as go-between. The reason he gave for ordering this ceremony, to others and perhaps even to himself, was that there was no harm in it; true, it was costing him quite a bit of money, but he was prepared to think of the sum as a donation to the temple, the sort that would earn one merit in some final reckoning.

It was exactly a year after my mother's burial service in London, and we had all found ourselves in Hong Kong. (I was there anyway, working unhappily but industriously at a job in journalism.) My father believed some sort of rite should be performed to mark the anniversary, it didn't matter which sort; if Ah Sam thought Buddhist was best, Buddhist it would be. Ah Sam, who had been around for as long as I can remember, is that familiar figure of the Chinese household, the queenly maid.

I turned to look at her. Sitting upright in a hard chair, with hands clasped together and a stillness conveying some sculpted figure, she put at a disadvantage the rest of us, who could not hope to endure the rites with as much composure. 'I'll just nip into the kitchen and see to the food,' she presently said, getting up from her chair.

'You mean the offerings?' I was a little puzzled, for I noticed that the altar, beneath a photograph of my mother, already held dishes heaped with an almost Lucullan prodigality.

'No, I was wondering about our vegetarian lunch.'

A vegetarian feast was to accompany the service. How, apart from eating, is one to mark an occasion if one is Chinese? I couldn't imagine any church in England throwing in a banquet with a memorial service.

I followed Ah Sam into the kitchen, which I found to be large and, at first glance, rather primitive. An enormous wooden table, grooved with age and glossy with kitchen grease, stood in the centre, and at this a nun in grey habit was hovering. She and Ah Sam greeted each other with a murmur of 'Amitabha.' This nun was, it turned out, Ah Sam's chief contact at the monastery. A former domestic, she had been taken into service by a family Ah Sam had once worked for in China; that was how they had met. In the Cantonese-speaking province where they both came from,

8

there existed a sisterhood of peasant women who, rather than submit to the common female fate of being sold into marriage with perfect strangers, took a vow to bind themselves to chastity. To earn their living they usually went into service. For this nun, as for so many of that sisterhood, the taking of monastic vows must have followed naturally enough from the pledge of celibacy.

I looked at the two women as they fussed over some vegetables. They were of the same height and age. Ah Sam's hair was jet black, drawn back in an immaculate bun. The nun, with her shaved head, should have seemed unwomanly; yet it cannot be said that she was. Her smooth face was still young, suggesting rose petals. She was perhaps sixty, but you'd never think so to look at her face. Leaving the kitchen, I remarked on this to Ah Sam, who said, as if nothing could be more obvious: 'It's the meditative life and not eating meat.'

The service began at the appointed time. Monks and acolytes took their places before individual reading stands, in rows. A little bell was rung and chanting in unison began. The voices flowed all over the hall, rhythmic and indistinct like a continuous throb. The monks sounded as if the noises were coming out of their noses instead of their throats. I could not help smiling at one of them, who interrupted his incantation to gulp tea from an oversized, flower-patterned mug from time to time.

My relatives and I all knelt on stools, and tried to follow the recitations from the books of sutras opened on stands in front of us. It was not easy, so many of the Chinese characters represented the sounds of unfamiliar Sanskrit words. To my sense of baffled and half-ironic detachment, the chanting of mantras, of talismanic Sanskrit words, was beginning to seem like mumbo-jumbo. Saying these masses was supposed to help my mother's soul across the Sea of Pain, the intermediary state

9

between death and rebirth, but while I like suggestions of fire and water and rebirth, I could not help thinking it was all mummery.

And yet, Buddhist notions are part of the thinking of almost every Chinese, even of unbelievers like me. The language I speak, the morality I was taught, the legends and fairy tales I was reared on – all these have been so deeply coloured by Buddhism that ideas like the transmigration of souls and of rebirth in the Western Paradise are familiar to me from childhood, unconsciously imbibed through phrases like *yinguo baoying* and Xitian – phrases that are rarely linked in my mind to their Sanskrit progenitors, karma and Sukhavati, because they seem so much a part of everyday Chinese vocabulary.

So it is perhaps not surprising that gradually another state of mind overtook me. It was strange, after a while, to feel myself entering into the spirit of the ceremony, when I might so easily have dismissed it, have asked myself, 'How could you sit through this medieval nonsense?' The sutras were now passing from ear to mind through memory, and given meaning by it. Perhaps it was only in my fancy that snatches of the recitation grew understandable, but I thought I caught these words to Amitabha:

Perfect master,
Who shines upon all things and all men,
As gleaming moonlight plays upon a thousand waters at the same
time,
Your great compassion does not pass by a single creature;
Steadily and quietly sails the great ship of compassion across the
Sea of Pain.
Physician for a sick and impure world,
You give in pity the invitation to the Paradise of the West.

I saw that even in an age of science and unbelief, our ideas are myths, mysteries, mere superstitions. And I found myself remembering, my mind going back to that time I went to see Mrs Jackson . . . I have not spoken of it to anyone, but it has haunted me ever since.

It was in London, after I had been to see my mother at Hammersmith Hospital. I was stepping out of her ward and making for the stairs when I felt someone touch my arm. A large dark shadow detached itself from a half-lit corner and assumed the figure of a Jamaican woman, who called on me, in a whisper, to stop. It took only a second to recognize her: she was a cleaner, someone I had seen ambling down the corridor with pail and mop during my daily visits to the hospital. She wore a nylon overall and had a tired, brown-black face.

She told me her name was Mrs Jackson, and she was sorry my mother was so ill. She could help us if I would let her. I must have stared at her or looked dubious because she said, 'It's all right. Trust me.'

She paused, then went on, lowering her voice further, 'I have something which may help her. I won't keep you now, but come to my house tonight and I will give it to you.' I wasn't to let anyone at the hospital know, she added, twice.

I am ashamed to say that my first thought was, Obeah. I had a vision of a cock with its throat cut and the blood falling drop by drop into a reddening basin of water. Mrs Jackson's sympathy, speaking to me out of the gentleness of her face, put me under an obligation to say yes, but to visit her at her home was the last thing I felt like doing, and I searched my mind for an excuse. I couldn't think of anything, and almost before I realized what was happening Mrs Jackson had thrust a piece of paper with her address into my hand.

The image of the cock was what kept coming into my mind as

I was driving home across the Marylebone flyover. I am not a believer in magic, and I didn't think for a moment that Mrs Jackson knew secrets or ways that could help me or hurt me. I was deeply touched by her concern and kindness, but I thought I had enough on my plate without having to contend with sorcery.

The minute I got back to the flat, the phone rang. A few seconds passed; and then a nurse at the other end of the line said that my mother had gone into a coma. I said that I would be over immediately. How earnestly, now, I wished I had said no to Mrs Jackson. I looked at the scrap of paper she had slipped into my hand with a sinking feeling; the address, in Kensal Rise, impinged on my mind distantly. I kept thinking I should have been ruthless with Mrs Jackson, but to stand her up now would be a discourtesy of which, distraught as I was, I was not quite capable.

It must have taken me half an hour to find her house. A young man let me in, then showed me without a word to the front room. Mrs Jackson was there, sitting on a settee, her feet rooted in unbecoming felt slippers. Lifting a pink palm, she greeted me: 'I have been expecting you.'

I only smiled and looked at the room. It had tropical-fruit-coloured wallpaper, floral chairs flanking a circular coffee table bearing Caribbean souvenirs, and a ruby vase holding roses whose never-ending bloom was too good to be true.

From somewhere behind her settee Mrs Jackson brought out a wine bottle filled with a liquid, pale brown like watered-down soy sauce.

'Be sure to give this to your mother tonight,' she instructed. 'You mustn't leave it standing; it is then not good, not good at all.'

I thanked her, then sat down, so as not to appear ungrateful by rushing away. It was strange sitting there in Mrs Jackson's colourful living room, stranger still to find her gently taking my hand, and breaking into a prayer: 'O Lord, there is no god like unto thee. As thou knowst not what is the way of the spirit . . . even so thou knowst not the works of God who maketh all.'

This strangeness was absorbed into a larger strangeness when she all of a sudden started to sing. She was singing a prayer for my mother – singing in what spirit, in what world, and with what faith I knew not, nor to which music. The everyday world seemed very far away and I could hardly believe I was in London, let alone Kensal Rise, and not somewhere many times more exotic.

Afterwards, as if a curtain had fallen, as if my visit to Mrs Jackson were only a dream, I continued my journey, turned now towards Hammersmith, where a person who had helped make me was already lost to me.

My mother died two days later. And now, in this temple, they were singing for her soul, appealing to magic and the gods just as Mrs Jackson had sung for her life in Kensal Rise.

While one half of my mind was drawing the comparison, the other half registered a change in the liturgical proceedings. We were breaking for lunch. The monks gathered themselves up and filed out. I watched as two high, round tables were brought in and bowls and chopsticks set on them. The monks came back and took their places at one of the tables; I understood that they were to eat first. They devoured the food quickly, making little grimaces and many sucking noises. Something extraordinary was that no one spoke: apparently monks are supposed to concentrate their minds on those who had provided the food, to regard which as anything other than medicine would be considered debauched.

Before they were all finished two nuns entered bearing dishes to our table. The dishes, in accordance with Buddhist dietary practice, were meatless and abstemious as regards such 'rank' flavours as onion and garlic; but they were in keeping with Chinese style, I observed, in their excessiveness. I also observed that beancurd, which is to Chinese vegetarianism what cheese is to Western, abounded (like cheese, beancurd comes in many shapes and textures; but unlike cheese, it is so bland in itself that it can be made to take on flavours with a chameleon versatility. It can even be made to resemble and taste like meat; and Mock Chicken, Mock Goose, Mock Abalone made from beancurd are common dishes in vegetarian cookery). My father, picking up a piece of beancurd from a dish of imitation duck, said, 'Men are carnivores at heart.'

I do not now recall if the circumambulations took place before or after lunch; this part of the ceremony consisted of a procession, with everyone leaving their places and winding about the shrine hall, then passing in single file from room to room, reciting 'Homage to Buddha Amitabha' the while. I only remember following the procession in its serpentine course, walking a few paces behind my brother.

The last event of the day was the burning of paper 'spirit' money and objects for my mother's use in the next world. Times had changed since burying a person properly meant filling the tomb with mortuary goods, pottery models of possessions such as its occupant could do with in heaven. Nowadays, to keep the dead in the style to which they had become accustomed in life, one commissions paper mock-ups of objects of earthly desire (such as a house complete with a three-piece suite, doll's-house furnishings and even servants). I was sorry times had changed, thinking of those wonderful ceramics archaeologists had unearthed from ancient Chinese tombs.

It was late afternoon when, following Ah Sam, I strolled down the path leading from the temple courtyard to where the burning was to take place. It was a cleft in the hill on which the temple stood. The treasure heap, looking highly combustible and somehow lonely, became a pyre; from a cloud of humid smoke, through which near and distant objects appeared to billow, ash fell plentifully. The others stayed only a few minutes, and Ah Sam and I were the only two to remain.

We were standing there, not speaking, when Ah Sam suddenly turned to me and said, 'A car.' Her voice sounded regretful, as though she were responsible.

'We forgot to include a motor car,' she went on; 'your mother drove one, didn't she?' With her Toyota missing, how was she to get about in the other world?

I looked back from Ah Sam to the conflagration, hiding my smile. I felt an epoch instead of a mere generation separated me from Ah Sam, and I also suspected that I was the poorer for being further cut off from folk and faith.

This talk of cars made me think of my mother first learning to drive. It was in Malaya, and the car she drove was a second-hand jeep. It seemed altogether wrong. The thing was, my mother was an elegant woman, a person of pampered indoor breeding; that was the great and touching thing about her driving us children so determinedly from house to school, school to house, under the scorching sun, sweat and dust mingling on her fine, fair skin.

But at the time my father could afford nothing better; it was as simple as that. He was a newly arrived immigrant in a strange tropical country, stripped of everything he had once owned and struggling to make a fresh start. To go from a Lagonda classic sports car in swanky Old Shanghai to a rusty jeep in the jungles of Malaya was indeed a comedown, but for people of my parents' class, that was revolution in a nutshell.

Our house had no electricity or running water. Mosquitoes stung us on face and arms; sores from infected bites scarred our legs. In the house ants crawled around cups, or carried dead upturned cockroaches or beetles away like pallbearers. Lizards darted after insects on walls, their tails sometimes dropping on to the table and into the cups. My mother taught her children to read and told them stories by the light of a kerosene lamp. She looked elegant still, but the hands that held the book were roughened. A daughter died, then a son, and all because the hospitals were inadequate.

Hard as Malaya was, there was no question of going back to China, or even of going to Hong Kong, *the* place for refugee capitalists from Shanghai, their second eldorado. After leaving Shanghai, my father had started a business as a stock and exchange broker in Hong Kong, but although this enterprise had flourished for a while, the skies had suddenly collapsed upon him. It is hard to determine what exactly happened; I think his partner, one of the many adopted sons of Silas Hardoon, the well-known Jewish tycoon in Shanghai, was at least partly to blame. At any rate my father lost a fortune, and bankruptcy was all that was left.

With no money to speak of, and a family to support, my father's position was desperate. He was prepared to try almost anything – even the backwoods of Malaya, about which he knew nothing beyond the rumour that there might be opportunities there. Malaya was 'South Seas' to him: going there must have seemed as final as a step into the unknown, a hazardous passage to another life, from which no one returned the same.

And so it proved. Going to Malaya, he buried at last his dream of returning one day to Shanghai. I once heard him say to a friend, 'For ten years I thought I would go back; for ten years I looked back, not forward.' In an old Chinese story you would wake after ten years to find it had all been a dream. Only this was history, and he counted himself lucky that he awoke to it before it was too late. His looking forward affected us children. In

England, where I came to study, I would be asked, 'Ever been to China?' And I would answer, 'Long ago.' China had become the long ago, the memory.

My mother's strength carried her through her uprooting. She did what she must. With that emphatic quality of hers, she grasped the nettle – though the nettle grasped remained no less a nettle. Her inability to find in her displacement and successful adjustment any cause for self-pity or congratulation was the Chinese in her; it is only the English, enjoying stability in their country for so long, who use words like 'courage' and 'dignity' of people who rise above the smallest dislocation. My mother did not cling to her memories of a lost land; her reminiscences of Shanghai were not a case of trying to call back her yesterday. Though I was made aware at an early age of how glorious life had been in Shanghai (was it Talleyrand who said, 'He who has not lived before the revolution shall never know the sweetness of life'?), that awareness was merged with a sense of severance, such as one gets from contemplating the world before a war.

What struck me now, standing by the ashes of my mother's 'spirit' possessions, was the completeness of that severance. The measure of it was the fact that she had been dead a year, and her own mother, living in China, had no inkling of it; indeed might never get to hear of it, if the wish was to spare her. In that respect the Bamboo Curtain was not a source of difficulty, but ease.

Simultaneously there came to my mind all those ads you saw in Chinese newspapers in Hong Kong of fathers looking for their sons, mothers for their daughters, sisters for their brothers . . . ('WANG SHUCHUN SEEKS SON TIAN JINFENG: Tian Jinfeng, aged fifty-nine, formerly of Dacheng County, Hebei Province, left with the Kuomintang Army in 1949 for Taiwan, and has not been heard of since. His mother, now seventy-nine, desires a reunion in the time left to her. Anyone who has news of him please write to Wang Shuchun, Songji Hamlet, Dacheng County, Hebei Province.') I have always wondered what the success rate of these Wanted columns was: did Wang Shuchun become reunited with her son? What if he was already dead? How would it be for her to learn from some stranger answering the ad that all this time her son's death had lain in wait for her discovery, an unknown and terrible loss in store?

The Chinese have learned the acceptance of separation as an unremarkable norm of life. Yet all of a sudden it seemed incredible to me that you could die without your mother hearing of it. I was thinking of my mother, then of myself; I was thinking, I could have died before you, there are only nineteen years between us. One is apt to think of one's parents as old; yet my mother was young to have died – too young yet to set store by her memories. Was that why she gave the impression of having done for good with that part of her life that was lived in China, as though who one is *isn't* where one comes from?

With this thought there came a dense tangle of many others, until the voice of Ah Sam broke in with, 'Shall we go back?'

I think it was at that moment that the idea of going back to China began to form itself and to stand waiting in a corner of my mind.

3

Working as a journalist in Hong Kong, I felt the disadvantage of my nationality, which at the time (1978) was Malaysian. Up till then, I had felt quite neutral about it: I didn't particularly like or dislike it. But in Hong Kong it began to bother me. Once, offered an assignment to cover the Canton Fair for a trade magazine, I was sorry to have to turn it down; I knew that the Malaysian authorities, should I be fool enough to put in for clearance, would advise me never to return to Malaysia if I so much as set foot in communist China.

I don't know when I conceived the idea of changing my nationality to British. One thing is certain: my sole motive in doing so was to have a passport to travel to China. Determined to see this project through, I returned to England and took up a teaching job at Cambridge University just so as to be in the right place for putting in an application.

I wonder now at my single-mindedness; a wait of years for anything, let alone for a British passport, would normally have been too much for me. And I knew, this being Britain, that there would be a long wait. Indeed, the notice handed out by the Nationality Division of the Home Office to all hopeful applicants said as much: 'Enquiries about the progress of applications (of which there are many) divert the available manpower resources from the work on considering applications and thus cause even greater delays,' paragraph 2 reads. The notice goes on, and here the words leap out at you in bold type: 'In future, and in the interests of all applicants, enquiries from applicants about the progress of their applications will not be replied to.' The bit about the interests of the applicants sounded especially ominous, suggesting that your enquiries would be held against you.

Fourteen months after my application had gone in I was asked to appear for an interview with a man from Her Majesty's Immigration Office, the purpose of which was to establish that I satisfied the Secretary of State on such matters as my character and knowledge of the English (or Welsh) language. After talking a bit about myself, I was asked my reason for wanting to become a British citizen. My interviewer was a young, bearded and most likeable man, very English in the self-deprecatory way in which he posed that question, his tone implying, Surely you don't want to live in this country, with its miners, bad food and ghastly weather?

Having decided to be perfectly truthful, I answered, 'To be British would make it easier for me to visit China.' If my honest answer sounded eccentric, I had also decided that eccentricity went down well with the British.

I must have been right, because three months later, and somewhat sooner than I had expected, I held an invitation to swear allegiance to Her Majesty the Queen, her heir and her descendants. My job at Cambridge having in any case come to an end, there was nothing to stop me from leaving for China.

Arriving in Hong Kong at the start of 1981, I scribbled a note and sent it to my father in Malaysia to say that in three weeks I would be in Shanghai, and I gave him the name of the hotel where I'd be staying.

When I landed at Shanghai's Hongqiao Airport, the air did not turn instantly tense, nor did uniformed communist officials order me with blank-faced belligerence to open my bags for inspection. The wraps of officiousness fell away from the young customs officer the minute he opened his mouth. 'Brought any presents?' he asked, smiling, and blow me if he didn't speak in my own dialect! This was no state functionary, I thought; this could be my brother. (Later, even buying a postage stamp in this city gave me a sense of secret intoxication, for I had never before asked for a stamp in my own tongue – Cantonese and Mandarin, yes, but never Shanghainese.)

I checked into the Hengshan Hotel, a 1930s building in what used to be the French Concession. I cannot now think what I expected from my stay in Shanghai; but one thing is certain, I did not expect the man who turned up at my hotel that first evening.

I had only been a short time in my room when my phone rang and I heard the receptionist say there was a guest to see me. Might he come up? She gave his name. I didn't catch it, but I said yes. I hadn't contacted any relatives in Shanghai or made my presence known to anybody, but for all I knew the Chinese intelligence service could have done all that for me.

One so easily imagines in retrospect that certain moments came with a sense of significance, when actually they have derived their meaning from later knowledge. All I know is that the appearance of Hanze – for that was the name I didn't catch – stands out clear from all my experiences in Shanghai.

From the way he spoke I'd say he was something over sixty, but his face seemed to have aged to nothing but a crinkled covering over the frame of bone and vein. He was dressed in familiar Chinese fashion, blue cloth outer tunic and trousers – visibly patched in two places – covering padded jacket and long johns. He was small, and his skin was browner than is usual for one from this part of China.

He greeted me with, 'I am Hanze, remember me?' His voice rasped, as if he had bad lungs.

I quickly stood aside to let him enter, gesturing at the pair of armchairs in the room, making polite noises to conceal my inability to place him. We sat down, and for a few moments I was mildly embarrassed. What should I say to him?

'So here you are,' said my guest, as if he had been awaiting my arrival for a long time. It was very odd to discover he had been aware of me all this time, while I had not known of his existence.

'You knew I was coming then?' I asked.

'Oh, yes,' he answered, and started to draw an envelope from a pocket. 'Your father wrote to tell me.' His manner was very gentle, utterly humble.

It had never occurred to me that my father would do such a thing. It was a measure of how little I knew my father that whether I thought him concerned or uncaring, to be genuinely interested in what I was doing or little aware of it, each impression seemed equally possible yet somehow false. Nor did I know what relationship he bore this man holding his letter out for me to read.

I recognized the elegant calligraphy at once: like a scholar's, you would say of my father's handwriting. Stylistically the letter was in the classical language, the Chinese 'Latin' that was his natural medium.

I began to read.

'My dear Hanze,' it said, 'This letter bears good news: my second daughter Ling arrives in Shanghai from Hong Kong on February 2 (Monday), and will put up at the Hengshan Hotel. You, Hanze, might have the great goodness to show Ling the old house at 116 Route Winling. I had in mind that you might also accompany her to the places mentioned in the attached list . . .'

The list began with 'Picardie Apartments'. I knew what that was; one book I had read, the memoirs of a diplomat in Old Shanghai, described it as one of those 'modern non-plus-ultra apartments' in the French Concession.

Seeing me glance at the list, Hanze explained, 'They are your grandfather's buildings, you see. The one we're in now, this Hengshan Hotel, used to be the Picardie Apartments, in fact. Quite a coincidence, that you should be staying here, in this building which the late master raised in 1934.'

The words, spoken as if the voice was a channel all silted from disuse, must have cost Hanze what it costs an inarticulate man to make a public speech. After a minute talk ran out again. Then, as I went over in my mind what he had just said, a memory stirred. On hearing him speak of my grandfather as 'the late master', scraps of reminiscence swam somewhere out of the wings of my mind and I suddenly remembered who Hanze was. A letter floated to the surface in me, as though whatever weighing it to the bottom had let go.

I had lived away from home for something like fourteen years before I received my first letter from my father; he never wrote to me, so long as my mother did, and the letter therefore came as a complete surprise. I was even more astonished when I read it, for it was all about someone called Hanze. I couldn't tell what had prompted him to write it, and reading that letter, I felt my father walk like a stranger through my mind. I have the letter still; roughly translated, it reads:

'There have been so many changes since the one which engulfed us and others of our kind in China. Unlucky though we are in our times, we have nevertheless survived the havoc of our fortunes well. I often think of those days which came between

23

then and now, and marvel at our great good luck in coming through them relatively unharmed. A gentle fate has been allotted each of our family; so far our lives have all been agreeably ordinary. We should count ourselves fortunate indeed, when ruin might have befallen us, or an even greater catastrophe. Though not possessed of great riches or great honour, we have been truly lucky.

'How different was the fate of Hanze! Do you remember him, our steward? He was no more than a child when he first came to work for your grandfather, running errands and helping around the house – you might call him an apprentice, that was the name one used then. He was well thought of by the family. He taught himself to read and write, to understand something of the ways of business, and above all to use the abacus. That became his forte, making calculations on the abacus. From his modest beginning he rose to the rank of bookkeeper, and in that capacity – as the trusted manager of the family's most intimate financial matters – he remained until your grandfather's death.

'Afterwards, when I set up as a stock and exchange broker in Hong Kong, going into partnership with a well-known British Jew from Shanghai, I sent for him. He came to Hong Kong, and took complete charge of my accounts. Those were palmy days for us both. I was giddy with success. But I was young. Too young. I lacked the experience to grasp opportunities when they occurred; add to that my injudiciousness and the untrustworthiness of friends, and you have all the makings of financial ruin: in six months I lost all that I had built up.

'Hanze saw it happen from start to finish, understanding everything perfectly, but saying nothing. I believe he saw the whole thing much more clearly than I, but not once could he bring himself to venture a judgement: to do so would be tantamount to his not knowing his place, and that was unthinkable. So he stuck by me loyally, unable to break the age-old mould in which the master–servant relationship has ever been cast. You would not have expected criticism from such a man, the proof of whose devotion to me was his utter silence in the face of my foolhardiness. In his acceptance of his master – the man as he was, with all the shortcomings of his youth and impetuosity – he evinced a loyalty you will not find easily in today's world.

'In 1952 Hanze returned to mainland China. He did not have a job, nor was he given one by the authorities. He scraped along, played mah-jong. For this the communist comrades sentenced him to slave labour at a camp in some remote corner of China. One can imagine what followed.

'In 1976, after an absence of more than twenty years, he was briefly reunited with his family in Shanghai. It was during this period that he took his courage in both hands and, through the intermediary of a friend recently given leave to emigrate to Hong Kong, made contact with me. We have been able to exchange one letter. Carried in different directions by two currents of time, we have yet found each other again. But in the interim a quarter of a century has gone by.

'He has another three years at the labour camp, but through his wife and daughter I may be able to send word to him, and perhaps in this way a little human warmth may reach him across the distance in the cold of his loneliness.

'When one thinks of the wheels of life, how they revolve, one is led to wonder if it is the times which shape our destiny, or if it isn't the deeds of our previous existences and the inexorable turns in the wheel of karma . . .'

There was not much more. The date, 4 April 1976, came after the signature. After reading the letter I lodged the story in my mind, and in time I forgot it. Or at least I thought I had. But forgotten things are perhaps the truest memories, lying deeper than those more easily nudged back.

Now, in my hotel room, I looked long at Hanze and I thought, There is so much to know and one can only guess; guess around him. I saw that his face, which made no demands on one, was free from appeal or suffering or any kind of challenge; he had rather the face of an experienced and trusted old family retainer, waiting with patience and understanding for when his services should be required. He had passed through some ultimate of human experience; yet you could not expect tears from this stoical brown face with forbearance written all over it.

He had a calming effect on me, and I thought what a good companion he would be for the days of exploration ahead. Hearing him invite me to lunch the next day, I quickly accepted. He said his wife, whom he called 'the old woman', would fix something simple.

When I saw him to the door he turned to me and said, 'To think that you were a mere child the last time I saw you. You were so small then, only this high. There was Moon, your nanny; and she was taking you children to your mother in Hong Kong. We sat in the waiting room at the train station, do you remember, and it was very cold?'

Was I really that small then? I couldn't remember. I tried to recall that journey, but the broken picture I summoned held only inconsequential details: the insistent whistle of a train; the little flashes of light as men lit their cigarettes; the guards banging doors; the warm, hard bodies pressing in the boat to which we transferred at Canton; Nanny Moon's voice calling me above the announcements and exhortations of the loudspeaker.

Our mother herself would be meeting us in Macao, Nanny

Moon had explained. Our father had got out of China first, then our mother; we, the children, were to follow. Only it was years before we were reunited. Though Mother had gone to considerable trouble to ensure they were not forgotten, by the time we left Shanghai our memory of them had dimmed. She would write often, giving us vivid details of their life in Hong Kong, but her letters were tenuous contacts, and from her absence I learned very young that the first condition of human existence is insecurity.

There was a bedside lamp in my hotel room but I couldn't get it to work. So I lay in the half-dark, imagining how the room might have looked in the '30s; and what, today, it might say to someone who knew it then. What else would the past yield, brought to nearer view by a gradual reliving? The full sense of where I was suddenly came home to me. I fell to remembering, and as I did so my mind formed a bridge between the journey conjured up by Hanze and a small incident which took place a few years before my arrival in Shanghai.

This was in Hong Kong, before my return to Cambridge. One day my father phoned me at my office, announcing he was in town for a few days. Would I fancy a weekend trip to Macao? He didn't have to tell me what he had in mind.

'What would I find to do when you are at the gaming tables?' I asked, feeling a new ease with my father.

'Oh, you could play too,' he answered, laughing.

We left by jetfoil. Macao lies forty miles from Hong Kong as the crow flies, on the western horn of the Pearl River estuary, some sixty-five miles downstream from Canton. No sooner did we arrive than my father made for the casino of the Hotel Lisboa. I left him there, in a vast room which with its blaze of hot synthetic light had the look of no particular hour, not day or night; and set off for a walk by myself around the peninsula.

'A Portugal-cum-China oddity', someone had said of Macao. The houses suggested an Iberian port, curving along the shore like smocking. I walked by baroque balconies and stuccoed buildings in pink, pistachio and faded ochre. I strolled along the Praia Grande, past centuries-old banyan trees. Macao is said to have more churches and chapels to the square mile than any city in the world, but the back streets made me think it was the sump into which the grease of daily money-making drained.

I began to make my way back to the hotel in the pause between afternoon and evening, walking quickly through the gathering dark. In the casino, businessmen, housewives, shop-keepers and, for all I knew, hawkers were laying bets with rapt intensity, shoulder to shoulder. The atmosphere struck me as being very different from that of the previous casino I was in with my father, a club in London's Mayfair where Indian women conforming to my idea of maharanees clasped playing-cards in jewel-encrusted fingers.

My father had seen me from a distance, through a screen of heads, and had crossed the room to intersect me. 'Tell you what,' he said as he drew near, 'I'll take you sightseeing.'

He hailed a taxi. 'Just drive,' he said to the driver as he climbed inside. 'I'll tell you when to stop.'

There is not much to Macao – not much more than two to three square miles in all, I'd say. Only a few moments seemed to have passed before we came in sight of the harbour. Boats, dim hulks in the darkening sky, lay this way and that amid flotsam. Yellow lights pierced the façades of the houses lining the quay.

'That's it,' my father said to me, as he tapped the driver on the shoulder to stop.

'What?'

'The hotel. The hotel where your mother waited for your boat from China.' We had both got out of the car.

I looked where he pointed his finger, and saw a narrow, rather seedy building standing within a few yards of the quay. Long windows with dark brown shutters gave on to the river. Music came across to us from a radio, and a young voice somewhere sang. As a warm, tropical breeze carried the smell of the sea towards me I heard my father say, 'When your exit permits came through, I had already left for Malaya. Your mother remained in Hong Kong, but she couldn't get you children to join her there – with all those refugees pouring in from China, visas into Hong Kong were like gold dust. So Macao it had to be; the idea was to get you here and then smuggle you into Hong Kong somehow.'

My mother didn't exactly know when we were arriving. 'On a tugboat from Canton, in two, maybe three weeks' time' was all that was known. She travelled to Macao alone, and took a first-floor room in an inn. It was seedy even then, with scabs of damp on the walls. But it had those long windows, and they faced the river. At those windows you could see the boats come in. She brought a chair, making a little distance between herself and the window so she might take in the entire harbour. There she sat, morning and afternoon, gazing down on the water and the boats chugging in. She kept her eyes open, even when the day darkened. How long was it before she spotted our boat? Five days? Ten? I do not know. The only detail I remember her recounting is of her burning a green mosquito-repelling coil in a saucer and laying it down at her feet. And I did not know, standing there below those windows with the taxi waiting, why that single memory should bring me close to tears.

'Something simple,' Hanzè had said of lunch, but of course it wasn't that. Had I been invited to a banquet I could not have been more splendidly fed. We ate winter bamboo shoots, tiny pink shrimps, chicken wings soused in yellow rice wine, ham from Jinhua and braised river fish. The dishes arrived one by one at the table and a good part of the meal was spent in making sure that I got the largest portion of everything.

The table at which Hanze and I sat was square and topped with a sheet of glass. Under the glass were placed snapshots, five or six of them, of his daughter Lili and her new husband. In the exact centre, wreathed by these other, larger pictures, was a passport photograph of my father.

The room was long and narrow, and though not large had been asked to accommodate a great deal. One end of it was entirely taken up with a wooden bed with thick cotton quilts folded carefully on it, and at the foot of this stood two large, old chests. In a corner stood an electric fan, still in its plastic cover, which Hanze informed me had been bought with a remittance from my father. It looked so important one nearly smiled. Above a cupboard there was a window, but there was no view, only the walls of buildings on the other side of the corridor of an alley – we were in what is called a *longtang* in Shanghai, a lane. Beyond the lane, across a street, are the hawkers' stands and stalls of the Bridge of the Eight Immortals, the food market from which many of the ingredients for my lunch had come.

It was obvious that they inhabited the one room. I glanced at it, and for a moment all I could think of was English country houses, imagining their gardens, their dogs with names, their flowered china and their open fireplaces. Much later I learned that Lili, who was recently married but who did not have luck enough to be given housing, lived with her parents in the same room, while her husband continued to live with his. I couldn't think how Hanze, his wife and Lili slept, the bed looked barely big enough for two.

After the first couple of courses, Hanze's wife Anfeng appeared. She was a bony woman, with a sallow face worn by hard work, anxiety and want. Her body looked as though it had been flattened between two boards. She bore dishes from the communal kitchen downstairs. I had passed that room on my way up, and I now wondered how such a place, so dark from coal-dust, so cramped, so unsuited to any kind of culinary endeavour, could have produced so splendid a meal. From age and traffic, the stairs I had climbed had deep grooves, almost hollows, in them, worn so smooth that I had to grip the handrail to stop myself from falling. I had mounted these stairs in impenetrable darkness – just electricity could be enchantment in this socialist city.

I insisted that Anfeng join us, adding that I was quite full and that she was not to cook any more dishes. I made a great fuss, to show that I'd be angry if she didn't sit down. As she did, you could feel the whole of her hesitate. She ate only rice, I noticed, and hardly touched any of the dishes. I kept having to say, 'Do eat, do eat some more,' as though I were the host and not she.

The meal finished, an enamel basin of hot water, a cake of new soap and a clean towel were brought upstairs. I washed my face and hands, and I was given to understand that nothing was too much trouble. I marvelled at the refinement, having noticed that water for the entire building came from a communal cold tap in the alley.

I asked Hanze, 'How did you come to live here?' I thought he might have been assigned this room by the authorities; instead he answered, 'When I got married your grandfather made it available to me, or at least to the old woman – I mostly slept over in your house.' He might have added, 'like any servant or drudge.' Instead he explained, 'It was simply easier that way.'

'You must have seen to everything in our house.' I had noticed that Hanze seldom took the initiative of speech.

'I entered the house as a dogsbody when I was sixteen,' he

said. 'One thing I did was to escort your father to and from school every day.'

'I thought he had a bodyguard for that, and also a chauffeur.'

'Yes,' he said evenly, 'but still your grandfather would rather I went along to make sure everything was all right.' Then, after the briefest pause, he added, 'Your grandfather had just the one son' – as if that explained everything.

After a silence he asked cautiously, 'Would you like to see something from that time?'

I was touched by the serious enquiry in his voice. On seeing me nod, he walked over to the cupboard and unlocked a drawer, then drew out a small packet wrapped in newspaper. (The newspaper, I was quite sure, was the only wrapping paper he had.) Nothing was said, but I could feel that whatever lay inside was something he held immensely dear. He unwrapped one layer of paper, then another; a gem of incalculable value could not have been handled with greater care and reverence. At last he produced it: a studio photograph, creased and tarnished, of himself and my father when young.

They dated the picture with their clothes, loose cotton robes with mandarin collars such as Chinese men still wore in the '30s and '40s. I made out Hanze's arm across my father's shoulder. My father's face, though absurdly young-looking, was instantly recognizable: it was merely the one I knew, divested of its adult features. But history had so worked on Hanze that the face which I now saw in front of me could scarcely be related to the one caught in the photograph.

'The Red Guards!' I burst out. 'Did the Red Guards not find this picture?'

How could he have risked preserving something so incriminating? I had heard enough about the Cultural Revolution to know that the Red Guards could do you in for a keepsake like this. Anyone could have told you it as good as damned you, this proof of your nostalgia for the Bad Old Days before the revolution.

'No, they didn't find it. The old woman burned everything else, or tried to. But not this; this I kept.'

He didn't have to tell me why. It was clear he could never bring himself to destroy anything so cherished. To do so would seem, perhaps, like an act deliberately carried out against the only value he could be sure of.

Looking at the picture, I thought how much I would like to hear an account of the intervening life, those years in labour camp. But that would happen in another place, and not for several years.

4

Here I was, in the most complete 1930s city that exists. Sheer crowdedness blurred and diluted impressions. Buses barrelled along, but few cars. Streets, once glittering with shops offering every luxury imaginable, were drab and bedraggled with people's ceaseless milling. I noted grimy architectural reminders of Kentish Town and Parisian suburbs and remembered what my mother had said on her first visit to London: 'It's so like Shanghai.' The place is scarcely believable, so easily could it remind you of, say, Liverpool; yet so Chinese the minute you plunge into the tangle of narrow lanes which lie behind the all but continuous buildings.

I wandered, taking whatever turn Hanze directed, watching the neighbourhoods change in some ebb and flow of their own. I was an explorer in my own native city, which was the more intriguing to me for being a place of excavation of my parents' past. It can't be true that it doesn't matter where you have lived, that you are yourself whether you are in Moscow or New York. I could so easily place my parents in that unstable compound of east and west which faced me wherever I looked.

Today Shanghai has more the look than the fact of European-ness. In one street, I was stopped in my tracks by a Russian

Orthodox church, beneath whose bulbous domes and cusped turrets I read a faded line of Chinese graffiti: LONG LIVE THE CHINESE COMMUNIST PARTY. This was set off by a tarnished picture in an alcove immediately above it of Madonna and Child.

Hanze and I were pursuing my grandfather's buildings. Nimble in his cloth shoes, Hanze walked quickly, picking his way down pavements thick with pedestrians. Above our heads, along the kerb, the stripped-down boughs of plane trees let through gashes of winter daylight where not blotted out by festoons of washing. I kept inhaling the smell of drains and an odour of burning coal. We were clear of the most crowded parts of the city when Hanze found what he was seeking, and stood to look at a walled house built on three floors. Following his gaze, I saw a flat roof and a series of cubes with metal window frames – a representation of the Bauhaus in China.

Three men rode by on bicycles, one taking his hands off the handlebars as he glanced in our direction, as if to say, 'Look, no hands!' Through grilles in the iron gate I could see the courtyard, asphalted over, and a single, leafless plane tree. A six-storey apartment block with balconies rose behind the house, sharing the courtyard.

For the first time in more than three decades I was looking through the gates of the house where I had spent the first years of my life. I was at the junction of Avenue Pétain and Route J. Winling. I was at my childhood home.

The shock was to find the past solidified – extant, not usurped by petrol pumps or serried racks of videos. I was struck also by that familiar sensation of homecoming: the surprise you feel at finding something smaller than you have pictured it. In my imagination I had revisited the house often. I saw it as spacious and comfortable, pairing Chinese fittings with European ameni-ties, and encompassing within its walls everything that was my father's and mother's early married life. A life which, in its singularity, was representative of all the singular lives in this world.

Trying to picture them young, I come up with two students attending courses at St John's, the American missionary university – he in Political Science, she in English Literature. He drove a 1939 Packard, very stylish with its long gleaming hood, its louvred radiator grille, its flaring front wings that swept down to the fenders and away, its leather seats smelling faintly of warm smoke. When not in their sable-lined long gowns he and his friends wore tailored serge suits, well-cut western trousers, leather loafers and soft cashmere sweaters. The girls wouldn't wear anything but the *cheongsam*, the Chinese sheath with the high collar and side slits, but they beamed out their consciousness of the latest styles from Europe in their accessories. In winter my mother would be wrapped in furs – brown beaver and cream lynx and leopardskin with its broken black rings.

My father had a cool indifference to books and classes, and it was the extra-curricular activities that captured the greater part of his interests. As new rhythms from America reached Shanghai there were long evenings of dancing on smooth floors to the music of Harry James, Gene Krupa, Artie Shaw, Benny Goodman and Jimmy Dorsay. Like any American kid, the dancers would move and hum with the numbers:

> *These foolish things*
> *Remind me of you . . .*

But they would only half understand the poignancy of lost love, these young men and women who even now were not above the conventional reality of arranged marriages, of filial obligations, of sexual relationships dictated by the old scripts.

When my father was betrothed, it was by parental arrange-
ment, my mother being the youngest daughter of a friend of his
father's. She was quite lovely, and a Lee. The name meant real
estate and a solid family seat in Zhenhai, near Ningbo. What was
more, her grandmother was a Fang, a byword for banking in
Shanghai.

I remember Great-grandmother Fang as a formidable lady –
old, very old, who never walked anywhere unassisted by her
maid because she wobbled so on her tiny 'lotus' feet. What it
meant to be connected to the Fang clan I discovered one day in
the University Library at Cambridge. In a book I happened to
chance upon there, I read a chapter by an American historian
named Susan Mann Jones. She was writing about the domination
of Shanghai's financial organization by the Ningbo community in
the late nineteenth and early twentieth centuries, and she had
this to say about the Fang family:

The most powerful and most prominent kinship group in the
Ningbo *bang* [clique] at Shanghai from the early nineteenth
century into the 1930s was the Fang lineage. As late as 1936,
an edition of *Who's Who in China* contains a paragraph and
biography of . . . the grandson of Fang the Seventh [the
legendary first founder of the native Chinese bank] . . . The
Fang lineage reinforced ties of kinship through the mainten-
ance of two large residential compounds in Zhenhai, where
members of the lineage lived and maintained ancestral
temples, and through the corporate ownership of various
business enterprises . . . At various times between 1936 and
1950 members of the Fang lineage owned seventeen native
banks in Shanghai, five in Ningbo, one in Hankou, and one in
Hangzhou.

The prospect of these banks opening to him was pleasing to my grandfather, who, as one who maintained that to succeed in business one must 'fly one's kite high' – which is another way of saying 'Who dares wins' or 'Nothing venture, nothing gain' – could always use some credit. He couldn't have been more delighted with the match. His star was already high when my parents married, and he was making considerable sums of money, but the likes of him took risks, now making a killing, now losing.

My grandfather's origins were humble – how humble I was about to learn from Hanze – but my father's genealogical inferiority was not a count against him. Though it was understood by some that my mother married beneath her, by most people (seeing the matter in purely mercenary terms) my parents were judged to be very well suited. I know that for my mother it was even a love match; she adored my father, who did indeed have a way with women.

An absence of materialistic yearnings in my mother attested to her landed background: she had evidently grown up among people who didn't need to buy things, whose contentment lay in having the money; whereas my father's family had the upstart's need to be lent importance by possessions.

The wedding festivities went on for three days and three nights. The glitter, the banquets, the opera performances elated the guests like new wine. There was deafening music, and a blaze of light. The wedding was by Chinese rite, but there were no prostrations before the parents-in-law, the bride being 'modern' in her upbringing. She had not even been taught to cast down her eyes, but when the couple had their photograph taken, she, who was almost his height, bent her knees under her robe to appear a little shorter. That first night Nanny Moon, my mother's nurse before she became mine, kept vigil outside the bridal chamber, then entered first thing the next morning to emerge from it triumphantly flourishing a stained sheet.

The year was 1943; the films at the cinemas were *Qiu Haitang* and *For Whom the Bell Tolls*, the one with Gary Cooper and Ingrid Bergman; the Japanese had occupied Shanghai for six years, and it would only be another six before one found everything irrevocably changed.

Nothing of the atmosphere of that time came through in the house that I now saw, standing with Hanze on Route Winling, or Wanping Lu, as it is now called. To discover if there were any ghosts I'd have to enter the house, and this I could not do, in a place where people were still wary and suspicious, and where the disquieting sensations of the Cultural Revolution still lurked. From the doorway there drifted smells of lunch being cooked. I heard the swish of bicycles behind me. I tried to picture the interiors – the dreary economy of underpowered electric light bulbs that merely emphasize the darkness; the rasping and clanking of taps unrenewed since 1937. From where I stood I couldn't see the garden where once was buried my grandfather's supply of opium, stored underground for the same reason one stores rice wine underground: to enrich the flavour.

Considering how little had been done by the present occupants to maintain them, both the house and the apartment block (the last building to be put up by my grandfather) had worn well, proof perhaps that they were built well.

As if reading my thoughts, Hanze said, 'It was Monsieur Minutti who designed them, you know, your grandfather's partner and close friend.'

I had met Monsieur Minutti, a canny Swiss architect working in the French Concession to whom my sister and I had been taken to have our heads patted at the age of two or three. Born in Geneva and educated in Zurich, the moustached Monsieur

Minutti already had Rio de Janeiro, Buenos Aires, Saigon and Singapore behind him when he arrived in Shanghai in 1920. He and my grandfather had a symbiotic relationship: they vouched for each other, he to the Frenchmen ruling the roost in the Concession, my grandfather to the Ningbo bankers who held the purse strings. They both knew how to allow the cosmopolitan character of Shanghai to work for them, and they got on so well that Monsieur Minutti chose to site his own house next door to ours.

We were at number 116; the garage with the Packard, Buick, Citroen and Lagonda was 118; and Monsieur Minutti's house was at 120. My grandfather built it for him, and it was understood by all concerned that he would charge only for the materials. They had done well out of the Picardie Apartments, which had been built at a cost of $2,000,000, big money in those days. Max, Monsieur Minutti's teenage son, became my father's best friend after my father gave him his first drag on a cigarette and introduced him to a shapely leg at a tea dance at the Paramount. (Decades later the two friends met up briefly in Geneva, where Max had settled into a job with the World Health Organization.)

'How on earth did Grandfather and Minutti manage to talk to each other?' I asked Hanze, as we began to walk away from the house.

'Your grandfather had an extremely quick mind. I don't think he had had many years of schooling, but he didn't let that stand in his way. He taught himself to read Chinese, English and French, and contracts in those languages never posed any difficulty. He used to carry a newspaper about with him, and you should see it after he'd finished with it; the margins would be scribbled all over with the new vocabulary he'd picked up and memorized that day.'

What else could he tell me about my grandfather? I was

curious to learn more. Over the next days, whenever there was a quiet moment, I asked Hanze questions; and from his answers I pieced together the scraps that made up my grandfather's life.

Younger by a decade than the century, my grandfather was born on a small island called Little Panshi in the Chusan Archipelago, not far to the south of Shanghai. Little Panshi was a place where nature had to be bribed to yield anything. But rural poverty meant there was nothing to bribe nature with – it was not a matter of working harder. The eldest of four brothers, my grandfather took the first step towards a better life by emigrating north to Shanghai. He set out on the road to the big city via Chusan, the island which, as the biggest in the group, has given its name to the archipelago as a whole. Emigration means failure, either the failure of the homeland or, for some, their own. Personal failure, given Little Panshi's, was what my grandfather could least afford; against it, he would have to pit all his diligence and daring.

Coming from the Chusan Archipelago, he was looked upon in Shanghai as a native of Ningbo, the prefecture that presided over all that part of the country. To be a Ningbo settler in the metropolis was no bad thing; the list of Ningbo people who had made good there was lengthy, and Shanghai had had its Ningbo enclaves and guild since the eighteenth century. (The domination of that association, named Siming Guild after the mountain range west of the city of Ningbo, fell into the hands of the Fang clan shortly after it was founded.) No big trade venture or commercial undertaking was without its Ningbo entrepreneur, and if my grandfather should rise to become anything in the world of business in Shanghai, he would be in very good company.

Until I learned the facts from Hanze I did not really know what my grandfather did in those early years in Shanghai. I had pictured an odd-job man, not quite a confidence trickster, but not strictly legitimate either. I had imagined him among stevedores loading and unloading the ocean-going ships on the Huangpu River. But I had, it seemed, romanticized his beginnings. It turned out that I am descended from a coolie.

In Shanghai my grandfather's employers were the British taipans on the Municipal Council of the International Settlement, the body that all but ruled the city. They were laying water mains and sewers beneath the settlement, and as a manual worker my grandfather was hired to dig ditches.

So were hundreds of other labourers, working in gangs under leaders. My grandfather observed those leaders, how they engaged men and kept track of the materials. He kept his wits about him. It was dirty work, his fingernails were a sight, but he was learning a trade, and he had no doubt that it would pay off.

The moment he felt he knew the business he approached the Municipal Council with a proposition: what if they sub-contracted portions of the works to him? The men in charge of the construction could see he knew a good deal about pipes and work rates and the prices of building materials; and they could tell a burgeoning entrepreneur when they saw one. He had one point in his favour – he was a businessman by instinct – and one point against him – he had yet to turn twenty. As his employers saw the matter, there was little about the proposition they could decently take exception to, and there was nothing whatever they could lose by it.

And so it came about that my grandfather became a building contractor. Shanghai in those days was a boom town, a property developer's dream; and Grandfather had met its ascent head-on. Even today the buildings of Shanghai could suggest to any visitor the confidence and boundless promise of that age.

My grandfather had a hand in raising quite a few of the city's most imposing buildings, some of them financial failures, others great successes. Many of them were in the French Concession, and of course he had Monsieur Minutti to thank for that. Hanze couldn't tell me how the two men met, but I had heard it said, I forget by whom, that my grandfather's stoop came of his having worked as a draughtsman in a European architect's office, and it might have been there that their paths had crossed. From the structures he left in Shanghai, I'd say that Monsieur Minutti was a 1930s modernist sympathetic to functionalism. I liked his buildings, with their clean lines and plainness. They had that sense of rootedness which is a mark of most good architecture.

Hanze amazed me by his total recall; he could remember to the last digit what the profits were on this venture, what the losses were on that. Of course his information was governed by his own notions of relevancy, but one thing I observed about him was his grasp of matters you'd think lay outside his interest and experience. He had, after all, been cut off from the world for more than two decades, and you would expect there to be some lacunae in his understanding. But no; whereas with other Chinese I constantly had to remind myself that what one person sees others view quite differently, with him I had the impression that such divergences were bridged by extra faculties. The feeling grew in me, increasingly intensely, that this man was my strongest link with the past.

I crossed the Soochow Creek by the Chapoo Road Bridge, which my grandfather built very early on in his career; on Avenue Roi Albert and Rue Lafayette I saw the Champs de Course Français (Canidrome for short), where greyhounds were bred and raced and which, as the dowdy Culture Square, my grandfather would scarcely recognize if he were to see it today. I stopped at the Grand Auditorium, just off Avenue Joffre, where *jai-alai* was nightly played to the sounds of the bookmakers shouting the odds and whose courts nowadays serve the Luwan Sports Centre. That my grandfather was no jerry-builder you could not doubt, seeing these structures. Next I walked along the Bund, the esplanade where the big business houses had their front doors facing the Huangpu River. Early in life my grandfather vowed that he would one day put a building on the Bund. This must have seemed a wild ambition, the Bund was so lordly, but it was exactly what he succeeded in doing. The tall building which once housed the Messageries Maritimes still surveys what used to be the Quai de France, the French stretch of the waterfront; and seeing it I thought, 'Not bad going for a one-time coolie.'

I tried to visualize those times, picturing the European tycoons driving into town along the tree-shaded boulevards from their spacious homes, furnished in the costliest British and French taste, and arriving at their brass-plated offices on the Bund, before tiffin at the club and cocktails at the Cercle Sportif Français.

The Chinese went about their business differently. Each time he landed a contract, my grandfather would go to a teahouse. Not just any old teahouse, but one known to everyone in the building trade. It would be in one of those streets off Nanking Road, and it would be astir with trading and bargaining. It was here that he signed up his sub-contractors, working his way up from floor to floor. There was one trade to every floor: the masons on one, the fitters on another, the plumbers on a third. He'd find the representatives of the big trading houses there too, so he would place his orders for construction materials as he went along. It was a time-honoured way of doing business, urbane, pleasant and decidedly efficient.

At half-past twelve he took his place at table, sometimes at a restaurant, sometimes at home. Once a week he took luncheon at the Palace Hotel, where he had his own table and where it was good to be seen to have one. It being known that money ran through his fingers when it came to tipping, he could be assured of obsequious waiters and unstinting attention.

From the Palace it was but a short drive to the singsong house. My grandfather was in the habit of looking in at such places and spicing his afternoons with the company of a cocotte or two. Chinese men, married or not, availed themselves of these traditional services the minute they could afford to. It must have been there that he picked up his opium habit, for in Shanghai the pipe and the bordello went together.

Did his wife mind? She was not supposed to. Weren't her fingers ringed by gold and jade where once they had been roughened by calluses? She was nothing but a manual worker when she first caught his eye, labouring to earn her living on a construction site. As the mother of his sons, surely she could feel her position secure, however much he might seem to prefer the company of those playthings of his? If he liked to divert himself in those singsong houses, this was only a case of a man having his way. It was not looked upon as anomalous by anyone; only it was the death of my grandmother.

5

It was the death of my grandmother, quite literally. I discovered how she died some time after my trip to Shanghai. Before that it hadn't occurred to me to ask about her, and in any case I had got into the habit of never asking my father difficult questions. There were hints at some unpleasantness, something more than one would care to speak of, but it wasn't until I had a chance to talk to my father's sister, the aunt I call Niangniang, that I learned what exactly happened.

Niangniang lives in theory with a married daughter in Sydney. Finding Australia dull, she would pop up so frequently in Hong Kong that she'd end up maintaining a flat there. I, too, was often in Hong Kong in the years succeeding my trip to Shanghai, years of extensive travels in the Far East. And it was there, over dinner, that I made her tell me about my grandmother. I remember thinking, as she told me the story, I will always listen from now on, to aunts, uncles, father, to anyone who will tell me things.

In most people, memories are worn thin by time, or else they are silted over by the events and weariness of years; in Niangniang, though, the spool of threads joining her to the past was found, when pulled on, to be time-proof. Incident after incident lives on in her memory. Old wrongs that in others would have sunk into forgetfulness are living in her still. For her, the past is as real as the present and continues to happen, and this is not only because she is old, but because to many Chinese what happens in history is not past, but all part of their now (and in that sense, China may be said to have no history). What's more, her memory is of a different quality from Hanze's, less precise, more obsessive, brighter but also harsher in colour. You never feel with Niangniang that you are entering calmer waters, only more turbulent. What was felt, suffered, comes through: the lightness in the head, the clutch in the midriff.

That day, she quaffed Carlsbergs and rambled, mentioning names. One was of a man in Canton; him my interest homed on, because I myself was headed for that city the next day.

It was work which took me to Canton, but one thing I was quite intent on doing in my one and a half days there was to look up this man Niangniang had mentioned. He is my father's half-brother, my grandfather's son by a mistress.

His mother was a woman of not entire virtue, called Bitao Laowu, Jade Peach Number Five. From the name most people in Shanghai would know that she was a singsong girl: that was the way they called them in the singsong house, Number So-and-so. As for the rest of her name, it was a sort of trademark; she was Jade Peach the way Clara Bow was the 'It Girl' or Theda Bara 'the Vamp'.

I may mislead when I say 'not entire virtue', because Jade Peach could very well have remained a virgin until she became my grandfather's mistress. She was alluring enough to be special, and special girls were saved up by the madams like treats. The exclusiveness of these girls was not only in their sexual immaculacy, but also in the fact that whoever paid for the privilege of deflowering one could, his means permitting, have her all to himself.

My grandmother knew all about Jade Peach, because after the affair had gone on for some time my grandfather had no qualms about bringing her home to tea occasionally. To take this without a murmur was a lot to ask of any wife, even a Chinese one. What was more, though Jade Peach was the favourite she was not the only one. There was Miss Di, Pearl Number Six. Pearl had not quite Jade Peach's looks but she had more of the feminine wiles. They both, following custom, addressed my grandmother as 'Sister', but the way she heard it they might have been saying 'Ogre'. I don't know how well Jade Peach and Pearl knew each other, or if they began their careers in the same establishment. Nor do I know to which of the six or seven grades of singsong girl they belonged – in other words, I don't know how high-class they were as courtesans. I always picture the ones at the top of the profession reclining on nests of brocade cushions and letting themselves get grossly fat from a combination of good living and boredom. I see creams and powders inside lacquered toilette boxes, and pairs of embroidered and beaded slippers under canopied beds. But I don't know if, where Jade Peach and Pearl were concerned, these images would serve.

My grandmother couldn't make a scene about these girls because her husband was apt to fly off the handle; once he threw a teapot at her. It was the tension in him, the edginess which came of always taking those tremendous risks in business. You couldn't really blame him if he was sometimes out of temper, and she didn't think she did; yet what else could it be but rage and reproach that she felt welling up inside her soul? There were occasions when she felt the day, the night, to be beyond the powers she had of living. There had been a few good years, at the beginning; but all good things must be paid for, either before or after.

From nobody might she expect sympathy, least of all from

other women, who, after remarking, 'Our kind know no choices,' reckoned there was nothing more to be said. Who was she to think that better was due to her? It didn't do to think of the old times; instead, she should bow quietly to Fate. To that harem resignation one half of her assented, but with the other half she contemplated the alternative. She saw another course opening to her, that of sinking into nothingness. Only that, she saw, could put the torment behind her.

She knew what she must do. She waited till he was out one afternoon before she made for his opium couch. There was the drug, of a finer quality than which you would not easily find in Shanghai. You swallowed two lumps of it, raw. You washed it down with a cup of brandy, neat. And there you were, dead. After she had put the cup down she lay back in her bed and closed her eyes. Other women before her had come at last to this.

When they found her her brows were drawn clearly above the thin, smooth lids, and her hair, black and shiny, did not have a strand out of place. Her mouth was firmly closed, the lips bloodless. Her pulse still flickered, but would not do so for long. She was thirty-three years old; her son, my father, was four.

Both she and Jade Peach had had two sons by my grandfather, but just as Jade Peach had lost one of her sons, so one of my grandmother's had died. No more than eight months separated the birth of my father and that of his surviving half-brother, but in almost every other way a chasm lay between them. Not the least of these was physical distance: the two never met as children. The childhood of Yeshu, as I propose to call my father's half-brother, is in itself a story, to be returned to later. Here I'll merely say that he was set apart, brought up in his mother's home town of Soochow, his very existence hidden from my father until my grandfather was on his deathbed and the two were already adults. As to what my father felt on having a half-brother sprung on him, this can only be guessed at; if his memory were a book it was a page he left uncut, not finding it tempting to read. I know that he went as far as acknowledging Yeshu as his brother, but I doubt if he went any further. It was not only that the two had grown up apart – and one loves one's own flesh, after all, the same way as one does anybody, through adjacency and shared experience – it was also that a shadow lay between them: the death of my father's mother, and the part that Yeshu's mother had in this. Also my father did not hold with the notion so much invoked by other Chinese: Blood is blood.

For a time the two brothers' lives were shaped by the same vicissitudes: revolution, dispossession, exile. When China went communist Yeshu moved to Hong Kong, where life as a refugee proved no less hard for him than for other Shanghainese, and days in which one prayed that something might intervene to save one – an introduction to a firm, a job, who knew? – passed with no offer of rescue. One did not realize one had so many unavailing friends until one was truly in need. The job he did finally get was not to do him much good, the company folding almost as soon as it got going. A place was found for him in my father's business, but that, too, soon failed, and he was left once more without any means of livelihood. It was at that moment that, through his wife's family connections, the prospect presented itself of a job at a branch of the Bank of China in Canton. Another man might have said, 'Anything but that, anything but going back to a country gone communist,' but he at that point could only see it as a chance to extricate himself from a hopeless situation. He left for Canton in early 1951, almost believing himself the patriotic new broom the bank was encouraging him to be. His wife did not follow until three months later, delayed by an abortion forced upon her by their straitened circumstances.

There seemed, that first May Day she watched him walk past in procession with his bank colleagues, red banners arching men and women, no case for regretting their decision to return, nor for fearing any future moment in which, out of the dark, the question might rear, Is there something about him, about his fate, that dooms him to disadvantage? For, one could not be at a greater disadvantage than to be stuck in China. One could not entertain the hope, as could those who got out, that one's hour would strike, however inauspicious the start.

Years passed; then decades, an interval of complete silence when China was cut off by an obsessive self-sufficiency and convulsed by the Cultural Revolution.

Now, after all those years, I was picking up the phone in the Overseas Chinese Hotel in Canton and asking for Yeshu at the bank.

Expecting bureaucratic unhelpfulness, invisible men shrugging their shoulders and saying, 'Never heard of him,' I was surprised how easy it was to find him. I only gave his name and he was put on. After I had said who I was I could hear nothing for a few seconds. I immediately thought it was a bad connection, but it proved to be only astonished silence, for afterwards his words came out over the line to me in a rush. 'Tell me where you are and I'll be over instantly.'

When he appeared at the hotel I was struck by his resemblance to my grandfather. He was as slender as my father, but there the likeness ended. I had forgotten to describe myself to him, but he had no trouble picking me out from the crowd in the lobby.

I went to his home and stayed for supper – noodles eaten to flashes of Premier Zhao Ziyang on TV. After all those years one didn't think so much about the original rights and wrongs; one gave oneself to the food and met the rest of the family. His wife was animated and chatty, delighting over a small grandchild. His daughter was quiet and looked long-suffering. Years later, she told me that until I turned up in Canton, she had no idea her father had any brothers and sisters, any relatives at all, either in or outside China; she had taken him for an orphan and an only child. When my mind went back to this afterwards, it struck me to wonder if there is such a thing as an innocent secret – isn't it to lend truth power to harm, to conceal it? Can a truth, neutral to begin with, not corrupt when it is buried?

They had a two-roomed but spacious flat in a row of worn brick houses with potted plants on the balcony. A comfortable enough place, by Chinese standards. They seemed to have done well for themselves, and the thought struck me that his family background must have helped Yeshu, for it defined him as a Victim of the Decadent Old Society, the sort whose lot the present régime had set out to improve. There was a quality of life – shabby yet punctilious, hard yet reposeful, sentimental, middling, mellowed in disillusionment – that one might find in any number of socialist cities.

As we were finishing our meal the son-in-law came in, and almost the first question he asked was if the digital watch I had given Yeshu's wife was an Omega (it was a Japanese make of no particular distinction). We talked a little while longer, but we touched on nothing important. Then it was time to leave. Everyone lamented the brevity of my stay; I must come again, they said, Canton did have one or two things to offer. My hands were clasped when I said goodbye. Out of worn, silent lanes I walked into a tree-lined pond and a summer evening in a big southern port: sultry, nostalgic, long. For a communist city there were quite a few lights.

*

In the telling, the story of my meeting with my father's half-brother seems unremarkable, the story of any number of Chinese of my generation. Nevertheless, for me, it was a loose stitch sewn up. It was as if, finding bits missing in a file docketed 'Grandmother', I had searched and turned up the mislaid pages.

That night in my hotel, I mentioned my grandmother's suicide to a colleague who had travelled to Canton with me. I said to him, 'You'd think she'd come to terms with it, wouldn't you, when it was no more than what many women in her day had to put up with from their husbands?'

He said, 'Maybe she was in love with him.'

And I thought: That's it! How could it not have been that? I recognized the truth of what my friend suggested at first flash. I then recalled how vague Niangniang had been, and how she had muttered something about the uncertainties of life in that age. 'Perhaps it was money,' she had added, unconvincingly. Nobody had thought to consider my grandmother as she was, a woman who felt herself wronged, and who wanted not to be tortured any more.

The crux of it all, it now seems plain to me, is that hers was not an arranged marriage. Arranged marriages, the bane and backbone of Chinese families, did not fall to the lot of two hard-up migrant workers; theirs was not a business of the family, not a property transaction with the partners' physical and material assets counterpoised like so many bargaining counters. So when the likes of Pearl and Jade Peach appeared, she was caught unready for the resigned acceptance that perhaps came the more easily to those who had not chosen their own husbands. Having married for love, it had never been intended that she waive her claim on her husband's fidelity.

Yet she was no better off in the end, subjected to no less humiliation than the rest of Chinese womankind. For completeness she should have had a tyrannical mother-in-law and scheming sisters-in-law, and she should have had to cope with a string of concubines.

When I think of the traditional Chinese family, I think of all the drama of the harem: the plots and the rivalries, the malice and the jealousies, the rumours, the unused energies channelling themselves into intrigues of breathtaking complexity. I have to laugh when I hear those apologists for the old Chinese family system who say that the wives and concubines lived together in perfect harmony and women had all the power, really – just think of those domineering matriarchs in fiction and history.

In fact the suggestion of discord was always there, the strain of breakdown and pain – only suppressed, one feels, by the force of habit or denial. And even the proverbial domination of the matriarch is little more than another expression of women's impotence, since it was entirely dependent on the production of sons and rarely sustained by anyone who was not prepared to devote to its attainment all her energy, skills and passion.

It was the boast of the Chinese that concubinage kept the family intact as a social unit, and was preferable to a permanent estrangement between the spouses. (Even in today's China, divorce is scarcely available as a retreat from hatred.) The question of how the women felt never came into it. No doubt many of them did not much care, one way or another; I shouldn't be at all surprised if some were simply numb – almost as if, having diverted or stifled their strongest emotions, they were left immune, feeling only the vaguest twinges of what might have been great anger or great grief. Only the few saw a solution in violent death. That is why, when my grandmother took her own life, people thought any one of half a dozen reasons more probable than a broken heart.

6

Around her open coffin in the funeral parlour, the mourners gathered. She lay straight and flat upon brocade, shocking in her stillness. A dead woman, a corpse. Around her a clamour had arisen, not so much of grief as ritual wailing. Her daughters and son were in the next room, sitting on the edge of chairs, quite straight and still as if they were having their photograph taken. Ying, the eldest, was sobbing softly. Niangniang, two years younger, stared in front of her, nerved for she could not tell what looming crisis. She felt that of the three, somehow it would be she who would always go and face the storm. Her little brother had hardly left his mother's lap, and had not understood when she told him that his mother was dead.

At intervals scraps of indistinct speech, all but drowned by the wailing, came from the adjacent parlour, separated from the children by wooden doors, through whose matt glass a light bulb shone yellow. Under the light, unseen by the children, Pearl was bending over the coffin and crying, 'Sister,' and 'Oh sister!', her white face expressing a kind of intent avidity. She did not perform alone; Jade Peach was weeping at least as inconsolably, and to the same shrill crescendo.

The doors opened and closed, admitting the children's uncle, their father's second brother. With a silent gesture of his head he signalled to the children. As Ying and Niangniang looked up he hissed, 'Go! Go to your father and tell him you want Aunt Pearl for a stepmother. Fall on your knees before him; do as I say. This is for your own good.'

They followed their uncle to the next room, Niangniang taking her brother's hand.

'Papa . . .'

They knocked their foreheads on the floor. In time, the two girls thought, kneeling side by side before their father, in time we will understand the meaning of what we are asking.

'Papa, we'd like Aunt Pearl for a mother.'

Their father did not answer; no muscle stirred. He knew his brother had put them up to it, and he also knew why. Jade Peach had already been twice pregnant, and fertility in a stepmother was something to be feared; she would have children of her own, and they would come before another woman's. Pearl was a different proposition; it was well known that she was barren.

Had he thought only of himself, my grandfather would have chosen Jade Peach, but it was Pearl he married, for the sake of his children. He assumed that Pearl would go on being just the same, willing, prudent, modest; her impulses did not seem to him to be intensified by any sense of urgency or vanity. The moments of misgiving as to the ultimate rightness of his choice only struck later, when he became aware of her determination not to let her new role overawe her; it was as if she recognized that to allow this was to underrate herself; as if she asked herself, What is the good of my elevation if I didn't make the most of it? That she became every inch the mistress of the house surprised almost everyone, not least the servants she began to order about. Her collection of valuable jewellery grew rapidly after she moved in, partly because she fiddled the domestic accounts, and partly because she was good at wheedling things out of her husband.

I think he must have forsaken his critical faculties when he took up with her. To me, her supposed attractiveness is difficult to imagine. How could she at any time of her life have been other than the dumpy woman that I knew? How did the young courtesan, whose business it was to please, develop into that disagreeable and vindictive shrew?

I don't think it is my fancy that invests her pictured body with an attitude of indolence; her chin drawn in upon its two or three duplications, she daily had her far from knotted muscles kneaded and tapped by one or another of the maids. Behind her back, and sometimes to her face, people called her 'Madame', pronouncing the word in the French way. They had the singsong house in mind when they used it, but of course the *double entendre* was lost on her. She never lost the manners of the *demi-monde*, and she kept up her connections with the milieu to which, as a country girl of fourteen, she was inducted when she first arrived in Shanghai from Soochow. When she raised her voice at the servants, she could have been any village woman in a market brawl. The way she drank tea, which was something she did endlessly, instantly gave her away, for she did it the way Shanghai's underworld characters do in books and movies – by sipping it from the spout of her own little teapot. My mother, whose upbringing could not have been more different, would shudder at the vulgarity.

The two women had to live under the same roof, but neither relished the proximity. My mother had modern ideas about almost everything – from food and religion to the way children should be brought up – and she clashed with Madame on every single one of them. Matters came to a head when, shortly after I

57

was born, Madame sent for a barber and ordered my head to be shaved.

'Her hair will grow the better for it,' she said. 'Denser and darker.' She was observing a custom which, unbeknown to her, could well have had its ancient origin in the need to control the spread of head lice.

'I've never heard of such a thing!' my mother exploded, and went home to her mother's for a whole month.

The effect that Madame had on my father, who was only four when she became his stepmother, was profound. He was, from the start, the tool of her power and domination. Where would she be today, she knew to ask herself with the shrewdness of her kind, if her husband hadn't wanted a devoted mother for his son? The child was her bulwark against possible rivals, and it was in her interest to indulge him and to make him the centre of things. So long as she had him, she could keep the likes of Jade Peach at bay. The favours with which she bribed him were as close as he ever came to a mother's love. I don't wonder that an obsessive secretiveness was engendered in him, and the habit of assuming a masquerade for protection. There grew inside him a sort of self-winding spring: the stresses of his childhood required compensation in worldly success; success entailed responsibilities, which in turn demanded further success. And so it went on inexorably, and I am not sure that the spiral could have gone on winding through the length of a normal life-span without snapping.

Madame commanded, fearfully, the ear of authority – the children's father. In this, as in her power to cause pain, she was strong. Niangniang was presently to know how strong when, the matter of her marriage having been raised, and a match-maker sent for, Madame intimated to my grandfather, casting aspersions on Niangniang's virtue, that it was best not to go for a social equal, in case one was handing over soiled goods. 'Like should marry like,' she said darkly, 'and if you don't know what that girl of yours is like, you must be deaf and blind.'

Niangniang did keep late nights, dancing and delighting in fresh experience – what fun-loving girl in Shanghai could resist its night-spots? – but of sex she knew nothing. Nor did she have any inkling of what was being planned behind her back. 'You must have liked your husband a little, you had two children by him?' I once asked her when she was nearly seventy. 'No,' she shook her head vehemently, 'I don't know what it is to love a man.'

She was always to call it a *mésalliance*, and to maintain that if it hadn't been for Madame's machinations, she would have made a happier match, or at least with a family nearer hers in wealth. The husband they found for her was the eldest son of a middling Shanghai family, a thick-set man, accustomed to having his own way since boyhood. She was not distressed to find herself harbouring uncharitable thoughts about him, and was less disturbed than bored when these thoughts constantly recurred.

That he was blatantly unfaithful to her was not unusual; what would have been unusual would be if she had minded. On the contrary, she was thankful to be spared the disagreeableness of having his hands on her too frequently. When he got one of their young maids pregnant, she felt a quick and, to her, unworthy pang, but it was less for the imagined carnality than because she knew it would fall to her to see to the practical arrangements – where to send the girl to have her baby, what to do about paying her off. For him she reserved the ultimate contempt, which was to excuse his misdemeanour as something native to him. 'Nothing but dogs,' she says of men.

She was too spirited and astute a woman to allow herself to sink into vapid domesticity, but boredom might have claimed her if she hadn't discovered the stimulations of gambling; for her, as for many women of her kind, mah-jong became a solace and a lifelong passion. She took refuge from emptiness in excesses, and her gambling losses were huge. But she raised her two girls with firmness, caning them now and then for what she believed to be their own good, toughening them for the uncertain times ahead. They were living through the tail-end of a civil war, and were soon to be doomed by a communist revolution.

Fleeing communism in 1949, they arrived in Hong Kong poor; Niangniang found she had to count her pennies, something she had never had to do before. She hated the pinched meanness of it all. It wasn't so much the poverty: a barefoot man is not poor unless he has always worn shoes. It was the humiliation, that was what rankled. With his weakness for a fast buck, her husband speculated with what money they had until it was all gone; starting with the huckster's hope, he moved swiftly to a bankrupt's lassitude. To make ends meet, many refugees from Shanghai, girls from once well-to-do families, were offering themselves as dance hostesses and mistresses; if she had suggested a similar course, she knew her husband would be craven enough to jump at it. 'I want a divorce,' she said instead. Better the stigma of a divorcee than the insult of being wife to such a man.

She had an admirer, a man of some means called Henry. Henry was kind, but shifty. It was years before she discovered that he was no import-export man but a spy for the Kuomintang government in Taiwan. Physically he was extremely unprepossessing, but the advantage of having someone generous enough to pay for her daughters' education was not lost on Niangniang. The sacrifice she made was not only that she felt nothing for the man, but also that she knew she had better in her. 'My capacity to suffer is not inexhaustible,' she was sometimes heard to say, this to forestall any criticism of her change of partner. The older girl was of an age to understand, and she matured quickly, becoming in time the most devoted of daughters, who has made it her first business ever since to attend to her mother's needs, extravagant as these are. Niangniang's eventual break-up with Henry was her way of letting her daughters know that she'd shot her bolt and that it was time, now that they were married and settled, they took care of her for a change.

'No,' she has told me more than once, 'I have never loved. Love is not a possession of one's own, it is something by which one is possessed.'

'Now your Aunt Ying was different,' she sometimes added. '*She* was possessed – and how!'

Ying was already making people smile in her teens; in full womanhood, she was a beauty. Brows with a perfect arc; skin of an ivory smoothness; cheeks faintly coloured, and not by art; lustrous black hair modishly framing her forehead – Ying had the sort of face that eyes were compulsively drawn to. Yet you might have felt unease in her beauty, not only because it invited plunder but also because of a suggestion of helpless vulnerability.

One day a guest came to the house to talk over some business with her father. Waiting in the drawing room for his host to appear, he saw Ying come in through the front door and cross the floor to the back quarters. The cut of her dress suggested a school uniform – he would discover which school from the uniform. She had hurried, and looked flushed. The rose of her cheeks, the physical immediacy of a tensed body, sent a ripple of desire through him. When she looked about her, she met his eyes; and she was not too young to grasp what she found there.

Next day, Ying found him hanging about outside her school. She resisted his blandishments, but not, I think, for very long; even if left alone, she would probably have been precocious. He'd seen that at once. He was the debonair sort one encountered at

the *thé dansant*, with something sleek and superficial about him,
a sort of charming carelessness. When he pulled her down, he
said, 'Come, I will teach you to like it.' It scared, and drew her.
He took her gently, there was no hurry, and she had not cried,
only winced a little. The fear she felt was then drawn away, borne
towards pleasure. He was a married man, but the realization that
he would misuse her had come too late, when she was already
trapped.

Ying's life was an illustration of the Chinese saying, She who is
beautiful is ill-fated. When her lover tired of her he simply threw
her over. 'A clean break,' she heard him say, as he left the room,
almost as casually as if he was going off to work. The finality of
those words shocked her into numbness, and it was some time
before she started writhing round on the bed, biting the pillow to
stifle her sobs.

You offer yourself entire for another's enjoyment, and if in the
end the gift is one he can no longer relish, it returns to you
worthless.

Afterwards, the grief wore off a little, but she had fits of
shame and misery, when she wished scarcely to live. Down again
and again on her came the enormous mortification trailing that
bitter question, Will I have to carry my disgrace about with me
for ever and ever? It was around this time that Jade Peach came
into her life. In other circumstances Ying might have required
more prompting, but when the older woman gave her some
opium to try, a few coaxing words were all that was needed. 'Go
on, it'll do you good. You'll forget all your pain.'

Jade Peach bristled with secret grudges against Ying's father,
and corrupting his favourite daughter seemed a good way to get
even with him. 'Nothing dreadful will happen to you,' she said to
Ying, 'you'll only feel relief.'

Relief? It produced more than relief; it exorcised her demon.

A few drags on the pipe, and the brain clouded, the emotions dulled, and a drowsiness was brought upon her which made all but the closest things unreal.

Days passed; all things pass. The next thing she knew, she was utterly possessed by opium. She became afraid, at those moments when she was not lost to everything. The reaction of her father, himself an addict, was: What I am, she shall not be. Wanting her weaned, he had the key to her room turned in the outer lock, even as he heard her childlike whimperings turn to shrieking from behind the door. He made himself deaf to her entreaties, but the thumpings on the door proved too much for Niangniang. She unlocked the door and looked in, and as she did so Ying shot past her and ran out of the room. The portion of her mind which stayed above the pain worked with feverish intensity, and she tore through the city, through the back streets, across the tramlines, not caring whether she lived or died so long as she could quench the scorching thirst in her body.

She was brought home limp and dazed, her craving satisfied for the time being. In that moment when hunger reached the climax of its violence, she had reached Jade Peach's house. I've made him pay, Jade Peach thought to herself, as Ying's screaming gasps and agonized appeals broke over her. It took two pipes to hush Ying's whimpering. Ministering to her, Jade Peach brooded on the girl's father: You bruised me, now I'm going to bruise you.

They could withhold the drug, but short of extremes they could not stop her from running away. Niangniang felt her stomach clench when her father spoke, more terribly than she had ever heard him, 'Get her head shaved.' He did not add, 'That'll keep her in.'

She was led into the room where the barber stood waiting, to see the table with the scissors and razor, and the maids and

Niangniang hovering. She threw herself at her sister's feet and clasped them crying, but Niangniang would not hear her, just hardened her heart and held her down, ordering the maids to do the same, till Ying began to feel the razor on her scalp and her hair falling, and she ceased to know anything except a cold fear and her own screams.

Baldness kept her in for a while, but her weakness for the drug was a wound that never entirely healed. She tried to suppress her craving, but it never really left her. In Hong Kong, to which she moved in 1949, she lived from day to day, and sometimes from hour to hour, for what they called 'white powder' in the vernacular. Only after a shot of heroin would she sleep heavily and long. She was someone gripped by a recurring pain, luminous with self-destruction. In the mirror she saw in her shadowed eyes the old woman she would never become. *'Help, help . . .'* she would cry silently to herself.

But help was not at hand; these days it was every man for himself; everyone was desperate, everyone a refugee. At night she could scarcely open a window without seeing a crowded pavement of sleeping figures, homeless exiles from China whose wretchedness was equal to hers. She seldom saw Niangniang, engaged in a struggle of her own. Indeed she knew no one who could be said to have his or her situation well in hand.

One day Niangniang followed a man down a corridor and into a room where an attendant briefly slid open a mortuary drawer and showed her Ying's dead face.

I learned from Niangniang when I met up with her in Hong Kong, where I came again to work in 1989, that Ying was buried in the Roman Catholic cemetery in Happy Valley. I bought a vase and a bouquet of lilies and tulips, and made my way there by taxi one Saturday afternoon. In the graveyard, where are laid the dead whom the living have ceased to cherish, white crosses and angels on pedestals protrude from burial plots pressed together with a tightness horribly replicating the warrens of the living. Half-way down an aisle, amid a cluster of speckled marble memorials, I found Ying's headstone. Her photograph was glazed on it, as were the dates of her birth and death; she died on 25 May 1953, I noted, three months after her fortieth birthday. In the eyes that look out from the photograph I fancied I saw a promise of passion which in another course of life might have made her the happiest of women.

In the bottom left-hand corner of the tombstone where the names of the bereaved are usually engraved, I could just make out the characters of Niangniang's name and, to my surprise, my father's, chiselled into the marble but with the paint long faded.

'You won't believe me,' Niangniang had said when I asked, 'but the news of her death came to me in a dream. A voice told me to go to a certain bus-stop. I did exactly that, and at the bus-stop I met a man who told me that Ying was dead. I then did what I must. I buried her as decently as I could, borrowing the money.' And then, from what she added, I concluded that my father's part in all this was negligible: 'His burdens were heavy at the time, trying to carve out a life in Malaya.'

It occurred to me, as my fingers felt the chiselled outline silently mouthing his name, that not once had I heard him speak of this sister of his. My mother, on the other hand, spoke frequently of *her* two sisters, our Lee aunts, each as accomplished and admirable a woman as anyone could ask for: 'Your *da ayi*, first aunt; your *er ayi*, second aunt,' she would say with obvious pride and fondness. But my father never spoke of his sisters in this way; indeed, of Ying he never spoke at all. Yet I know she was not forgotten. Once, sent to get him a handkerchief from his bedroom, I rummaged in a drawer and came upon a photograph. It showed the slab of a grave, and a headstone with inscriptions too small to decipher. I put it back where I'd found it, and said nothing to Father. I was perhaps thirteen or fourteen at the time, and it is only now that I make the connection, that I see clearly the lettering I could not read from the photograph.

7

For a good many years, whenever my grandfather celebrated his birthday, the King of Beggars would come to the house to wish him a long life. The King of Beggars was no pauper, but a swell who was often to be seen around town wearing a long silk gown and Bata leather shoes that could do with a more thorough polish but which gleamed in the instep. He looked a man with a place in society, not just someone at the top of a dunghill. He would come bearing gifts – perhaps boxes of sweetmeats wrapped in paper of the deepest crimson, perhaps some tins of rare teas. He would bow and utter effusive congratulatory phrases, conventional but heartfelt. Like all well-wishers he would be served the immemorial birthday food, noodles whose length betokens longevity.

There, he would say to himself as he took his leave, that's another year's good will renewed. The thought consoled him amid his cares; since the catastrophic siege of Shanghai in the summer and autumn months of 1937, the Japanese had enveloped the city, and the tens of thousands fleeing fire and shrapnel (or simply the odiousness of the army of occupation) to the sanctuary of the foreign concessions had confronted him and his fellow-beggars with a good deal of competition.

The years ahead promised every kind of confusion and uncertainty, so there was all the more reason for belonging to a guild or a gang and having leaders like himself to take thought for you. Those who at first had begrudged him his cut of their takings had soon learned better; Shanghai was no place for the freelance beggar.

My grandfather was one of his biggest and best clients in Frenchtown, regular with his payments, a man of his word. To the question as to whether *he* did right by his client, the King of Beggars would give an unhesitating 'Yes.' Let my grandfather ask himself how he would like it if his car were scratched the minute his chauffeur's back was turned, or if beggars beset him in droves whenever he stepped out of a street doorway. By paying his dues, he was sheathed against such nastiness.

Both men knew it to be a time-honoured Shanghai custom, protection. There was no getting away from it; it didn't matter who you were, up at the top of the social heap or down at the bottom. Not even the King of Beggars himself was immune. If anyone should grumble to him that he was expensive, he would counter the complaint with, 'Ah, but think of my costs, my overheads' – having in mind the monthly fees he paid the underworld gentry, the people who safeguarded his precinct from interlopers. To pledge or not to pledge your allegiance to a secret society was not for you to say – not in Shanghai, where a surge of crime signified not so much a lapse in policing as a breakdown in gangland order. Joining a secret society, the King of Beggars would say, puts you on an altogether better footing in any tussle over territory; and heaven knows there is enough rivalry.

Many were the violent events that might come upon you without warning. The car that crept up behind you, its yellow lights shining out in the darkness, could be carrying your murderers or, at best, your kidnappers. Of course kidnapping was a Shanghai speciality and you might well shrug, So what's new? But there *was* something new to today's violence: previously merely criminal, it had now a sinisterly political meaning; its connection with the Japanese military was both obvious and deeply disturbing. Now people had to take account of something more; now there was the terrorism wreaked upon each other's agents by the Chinese government and the Japanese Imperial Army.

By a mixture of bribery and coercion, agents of the Japanese Army were busily tempting men to collaboration, finding their takers among Kuomintang careerists, businessmen and gangsters. They found their Pétain in a sad but beguiling individual named Wang Jingwei, second to only Chiang Kai-shek in rank and stature in the Kuomintang. Him they installed at the head of a puppet régime in Nanking; but in so far as he and his hangers-on did any governing, they did it out of the Badlands of Shanghai.

The Badlands lay in the city's western district, crossed by the Great Western, Jessfield, Yu Yuan and Edinburgh Roads. For all practical purposes the area was an extension of the International Settlement, taxed and policed by the settlement's British authorities. Theoretically, though, the Chinese had never relinquished their rights to it – the area was *in* Chinese territory, you might say, but not *of* it. The British, who had their military barracks there, did not exactly write it off when the Chinese parts of the city all fell to the Japanese, but the Japanese were able to have their way with it, setting up a terrorist and spy ring at 76 Jessfield Road, and turning the place into a resort of secret agents, hired assassins, racketeers and gangsters.

For a time it was the fate of many Chinese who went over to the enemy to be gunned down by the Kuomintang's agents, or jerked out of their sleep and axed to death in their beds. By such acts of terrorism was it brought home to collaborators that it didn't pay to be on the wrong side. But then it didn't always pay to be on the right side either: you could bank on the Japanese secret service retaliating, and in kind – they had enough thugs in their pay for that. They certainly gave as good as they got, to judge from the severed head of a resistance fighter that might appear on a telegraph pole, or a chopped-off finger arriving anonymously in the post. It was almost as if the two sides had worked things out together, had agreed to maintain a balance of terror: if you dispatch one of ours, one of yours shall die; if it's a banker you bumped off, a banker is what we'll get next.

Awkwardly for the Japanese, the Kuomintang had Du Yuesheng on their side. Du was the underworld supremo, the godfather of Shanghai. Having him on your side must be like having Luchese, Bonnano, Genovese, Colombo and Gambino, all five of them, behind you in New York. His word alone was enough to end a war. His hitmen weren't just hitmen: they were soldiers of the underground resistance who terrorized those Chinese that chose to go over to the Japanese side and protected those that chose not to. At a word from one of them, a traitor could be intimidated enough to do a convulsive about-face. These people could make your nerves feel the assassin's blade dozens of times before it struck.

Crime alone couldn't have created the aura of Du Yuesheng. His businesses weren't just mob ones any more; they weren't just opium, gambling and racketeering. Indeed he was the first Chinese gangster to launder his money, the first to open a bank and to become a director of the Shanghai Stock Exchange, to sit on the board of the Chamber of Commerce and the French Municipal Council. What was more, he had long discovered the persuasion of money in political circles. There were times when Chiang Kai-shek himself felt uncomfortably in his power, and in deep. Du, after all, had been midwife to the Kuomintang's supremacy through its embattled beginnings.

That was back in 1927, the year of the workers' putsch. Had Du not forestalled it, a revolutionary workers' government might conceivably have formed, an urban soviet that might then have sparked off uprisings elsewhere in China, as had happened in the Bolshevik Revolution in Russia. Du was the one who, by setting the Green Gang upon the communists and unions, brought the Shanghai Spring to its bloody end and cleared the way for Chiang Kai-shek's takeover of the city. But for Du, Chiang Kai-shek might have had to share power with the communists. So Du had reason to complain of the ingratitude of Chiang. It pained him not a little that, except when he needed Du's services, Chiang was apt to snub him. Chiang didn't like to be reminded of his underworld connections; nor did he like the rich particularly: he liked riches better.

No, crime did not bound Du's horizon. The nefariousness of his opium cartel has been harped on by historians to the point of tedium, but no matter how you chip at his legend, Du Yuesheng remains Du Yuesheng in the popular imagination, the image of his iniquity balanced by heroism and patriotism.

My grandfather became a 'disciple'; that is to say, he underwent a ceremony in which he swore fealty to Du Yuesheng. For the dues he paid, he could expect a certain amount of protection – how else was one to be assured of a minimum of harassment in one's business dealings? To be patronized by Du Yuesheng was to signal 'Hands off' to one's enemies.

The one tangible memento of the occasion, a formal photograph, is long lost. This I learned from Hanze. I had not known any of it before I went to Shanghai; I began to find out the afternoon I visited an uncle of my mother's and found myself included in an invitation to a dinner party at the Jing'an Hotel that evening. The host, I learned, was a close friend of my great-uncle's son. I demurred at first, thinking myself a gatecrasher.

'After all, he doesn't know me,' I said to my great-uncle.

'Oh but he does. He knew your grandfather, and that's plenty good enough.'

The party was in a private room, an old-fashioned one with the agreeable faded opulence of a pre-war ballroom about it. The food stopped just short of magnificent, the helpings were over-generous. The guests looked so sleek I would not have known I was with men and women who had lived through the Cultural Revolution. Not to seem too bourgeois, I had put on an old jumper and a pair of grey corduroy trousers, and I was mortified to find myself the worst-dressed person in the room – I, the one representative of capitalist riches. Gazing round at the room I thought, amused: Of all the people here, I alone look the picture of political undeviation. My host, who lacked any particular physical distinction aside from bigness, had on a padded jacket of black embossed silk. He looked the sort of person to whom the maître d'hotel of an older day would say, 'I shall tell the chef *you* are here, sir.' For completeness, he should have been chewing a cigar. His wife exuded poise and good breeding and had clearly been a ravishing beauty.

'Would you be wanting to go to the opera while you're here?' my great-aunt asked me when we were into our fifth or sixth course.

'Yes, of course I would, but I gather tickets are very hard to come by at short notice.'

'Get Papa Du to help you. All doors open for Papa Du.' She smiled knowingly at our host, who at that moment was taking a cup of rice wine to his lips.

I suppressed my instinctive desire to gasp. All at once I realized who my host was. I had not thought it possible that the son of Old Shanghai's number-one gangster, the son, moreover, of one who had the blood of so many communist revolutionaries on his hands, would still be sitting pretty in People's China. One would have thought the new leaders would want to collect their blood debt, to pay off old scores. That Du Yuesheng was the Green Gang chief was the least of it; there was his intimacy with Chiang Kai-shek, the part he played in the crushing of the workers' movement in 1927 and the blood-letting of the ensuing White Terror. You couldn't live down family history like that.

Unless – and I suspect that that was the case – reputation weighed with the communists. As a victorious revolutionist might spare a king, so did the communists leave the pre-revolution big potatoes alone. Life had clearly left my host more than a little room for manoeuvre – if all doors, as my great-aunt had put it, opened for him. Most probably he was as much protected and guarded by the tacit acquiescence of the communist authorities as by their half-respectful mistrust. Who knows, it may well be true what rumour had once suggested, that Mao Zedong himself wanted Du Yuesheng for an ally in the takeover of Shanghai. Mao knew it would put the key to the city in his hand.

My grandfather had done the proper thing then, pledging himself to Du Yuesheng. It was not just a matter of lip-service either. To show good faith, my grandfather sent his son for a while to Zhongshi, the middle school established by Du Yuesheng in 1931, in the French Concession. Du's own sons went there, escorted to and fro by White Russian bodyguards. All the boys chafed against the discipline, which was tough. Too tough, it would seem, for my father, who was not there long before he was expelled; he'd got into a fight with a classmate and had cracked the poor boy's head.

One fascination, for me, of the time of which I speak is the way the underworld and the upperworld intermingled. One might think that my mother's family, being Old Money, would jib at consorting with a gangster; but no, Grandmother Lee, sweet-natured, gentle, guileless Grandmother Lee – even that most upright and virtuous of creatures was a frequent guest at Du Yuesheng's opera soirées. She and Du were both great devotees of Peking opera; two of his four wives were opera singers, famous ones at that. Opera, together with mah-jong and the opium pipe, was his relaxation, though it is hard to see how he had time for it.

All this was before hints of Japanese machinations forced him to decamp to Hong Kong – he was afraid that the Japanese might be plotting his doom and he preferred to take no chances. He left behind him an unease seeping even through the foreign districts, a city beset by new adversities, deeper forms of inner and outer want, and a surface brightness and gorgeousness, a sort of reeling phosphorescence that hid the nervousness and shrivelling within.

My grandfather had only just signed the contract for the Messageries Maritimes building on the Quai de France when hostilities engulfed Shanghai. There was nothing for it but to go ahead. Cement, stone and other building materials, harder and harder to come by, had to be imported from Vietnam; the Messageries Maritimes was just in time to ship them in before the Pacific blockade disrupted navigation. Though he did so in the teeth of soaring costs, Grandfather did make money on this venture, Hanze said. All the same it was to be his last big construction job; for, with a war on, who in his right mind would want to put up showpieces?

Not altogether surprisingly he branched out into new lines of business at this stage. He was nothing if not adaptable – the true immigrant entrepreneur. He flung himself into starting a tannery

and leather-goods factory; and as a sideline cultivated mush-
rooms (in greenhouses fitted with the most up-to-date instal-
lations for thermostatic control, Hanze thought it necessary to
emphasize when he related all this to me), finding his best
customers in Shanghai's Cantonese restaurants. Wartime might
not seem the best time for new ventures, and yet, though a good
many factory owners did indeed choose to close down or even
dismantle their plants (the ones that survived the bombing and
fighting), or to transfer them to the unoccupied areas in inland
China, the ledgers of the industrial and commercial enterprises
registered swift and distinct recovery a couple of years into the
occupation. Fortune seemed to smile on Shanghai's manufac-
turers at just the moment everything appeared about to be swept
away, and they were more than able to balance their books with
the bonanza of capital infusions from the interior and a suddenly
expanded pool of cheap labour, those lava tides of refugees with
their baskets and bundles, thronging the streets and the factories,
hungry, desperate, grateful to work for a song.

Meanwhile rumours, the by-product of war, circulated in the
city, the horror stories out of the Badlands, the scandals of
Japanese depredations and venality. One gave my grandfather
particular cause for worry, the rumour that Chinese opium
smokers were being blackmailed by the Japanese military. In fact
the Japanese and their puppets themselves peddled opium and
morphine; it was no secret that the Japanese Army's special
services made up the shortfall between their allotted funds and
their actual expenses by trafficking in narcotics and racketeering.
Yet these were the very people who blackmailed Chinese addicts
and preyed on their nerves. My grandfather's addiction, his
vulnerability, baulked him of the hope that he would say to the
Japanese, 'You have no hold over me.'

*

Pearl Harbor. Talk was of nothing else. You heard it at the club, in the teahouse, on golf courses. So much for the immunity of the foreign concessions. Hanze had picked up a leaflet, dropped by a Japanese plane, announcing the Declaration of War by His Imperial Japanese Majesty on the United States and Great Britain. At 10 a.m. sharp that drizzly morning, Japanese soldiers, long omnipresent in areas surrounding its boundaries, had entered the International Settlement, and were soon to be seen patrolling its streets, neutral territory no more.

It didn't mean much that they spared the French Concession, because France had already parted with much of its authority and independence. The concession had been under the jurisdiction of the Vichy government for well over a year now, French troops had been withdrawn from part of the concession's defence perimeter, and an accord had been signed between France and Japan the effect of which was to extend the influence of Wang Jingwei's regime in the foreign areas.

All this *wasn't* just so much history – this I was to learn many long years later from Hanze; unapprehended by him at the time, what happened then would set the course of his later life.

The effects of Japanese aggrandizement reached my grandfather soon enough, and in an increasingly fearful way. One day, a couple of Japanese Army officers appeared at the tannery and barked an order for boots, belts, straps and leather overcoats; and my grandfather knew, knew in his bones, that his business was done for as a money-making concern. No, they said, making stiff ushering gestures, as if to hasten the filling of the order, he was not to close it down either; the factory would continue to run, but under Japanese direction.

My grandfather had thought to give the Japanese a respectful berth, but just his wealth was enough to bring him to their attention. Nor did they think they had exhausted his possibilities when they got his factory to work to their specification; they reckoned they could squeeze more out of him, they had methods enough. Stories of their shakedowns were not in the least bit apocryphal, and their reputation for rapacity was founded on solid fact. Who has not heard tales of the Badlands? Yet because one never expects the laws of probability to apply to oneself, my grandfather was more incredulous than frightened when, as he walked towards his car through Avenue Joffre one scorching July day in 1942, two strangers burst from their hiding places and blocked his way. In a trice his arms were pinioned, his mouth gagged, but it wasn't until his captors had bundled him into a car that he realized he had·been kidnapped.

My father, just turned twenty, had never in his life felt so alarmed and frantic. When the news was brought to him, he saw, in his mind's eye, not the severing of ear, hand, or even head, but Grandfather collapsed, reduced, put through a range of ingenious tortures climaxed by the abrupt withdrawal of opium. He imagined diarrhoea, vomiting, fever, spasms, delirium – what they call a cold turkey.

Day after day passed while my father tried to discover his father's whereabouts. Hanze left on a four-hour train journey to Hangzhou on the track of a Japanese my father knew there, an adviser to the Imperial Army who might be persuaded to intercede. But the man was nowhere to be found, though Hanze explored every avenue. Meanwhile my father raked his friends and relatives for contacts. It was after ten fruitless days had passed that Zulai's name came up; if any man can help you, my father was told, he is the one.

Zulai was the youngest of my mother's six uncles. He was not universally admired or respected, having got considerable pleasure and profit from life by a complete disregard for honourable reputation. Indeed he considered only his own inclinations when, in the face of his mother's vehement objections, he took up with Danu. It was terrible to Great-grandmother Fang that a son of hers should abandon wife and child for a woman of the Danu sort, the sort for whom lovers were simply rungs on the social ladder. Like many a young woman who had passed her girlhood in the singsong house, Danu was known for her strong aspirations. A man could leave her, but this woman he would leave at a place higher than where he had found her. Zulai was perhaps the second or third rung; that there could be a fourth and fifth remained a theoretical possibility up until the revolution, which left her with fewer irons in the fire. Danu's mistakes were few – their annoying fewness may have accounted for her not being widely liked – but with Zulai, I think, she miscalculated; for though she won him and kept him, his mother spoiled things by disowning him.

(When I met her many years later in Hong Kong, I peered to see if the years had webbed her famously pearly skin, if cream and powder had silted into the pores. But no, the alabaster beauty was there still. Perfectly statuesque, with a *look* of scentedness about her, Danu would then have been, by my reckoning, just a few years short of seventy. She could have made heads turn even then. *He*, with his slightly crooked mouth, would not have stood out anywhere, young or old. I remember what they said of Danu in Shanghai, that unless the hour were dusk she never ventured outdoors, for fear of exposing her skin to the sun's wizening and darkening rays. Afraid of acquiring squint lines at the outer corners of her eyes, she always wore tinted glasses. She was no less concerned for her mouth; I have heard it said that the reason she never pursed her lips, or laughed generously, or smiled broadly, was that she was terrified that such muscular exertions would put tucks in the skin around her lips.)

Zulai, in spite of having been written off by his mother, could none the less count on her family connections to propel him into money-lending and now held a not unimportant job at a bank. For not holding out against the Japanese – against collaboration, you could have as easily said – he was soon to rise in his career. This was not opportunism, merely cynicism. Bad as it felt to be called a quisling, it was worse to be self-denying. In no time at all he would be working as a bank manager, and working as little as possible. (He died an American citizen, in Carmel, California, I believe. Before that he was often to be seen in Taipei and occasionally in Hong Kong – 'on business', he would say if anyone should ask. What business? My father's guess was CIA; Zulai might have no known job, but one did not imagine that he would go home in the afternoon to sleep or watch television.)

He was in a position to help, yes, he knew some people. He mentioned Wu Sibao, a name to make many blanch. Wu Sibao was not exactly a member of Wang Jingwei's government, but his name was inseparable from the lurid reputation of 'Number 76', the popular shorthand for the chamber of horrors at 76 Jessfield Road. Number 76 was where Wu Sibao hung out. At Number 76 the worlds of the secret service and secret society mingled – a common enough combination – and it was hard to tell what it was that Wu expended his considerable energies on, organized vice, espionage, or the third degree. A water seller to begin with, then a chauffeur, Wu Sibao now kept going on shakedowns. It was to such a man that my father must make his appeal.

He fully expected to hear screams as he approached Number 76, but all was quiet as he went through its arched entrance and ascended the steps to the doorway. Zulai had prepared the ground and, money having changed hands, had phoned my father to say that Grandfather could be collected that afternoon. My father had been compelled to say nothing to anyone; if he spoke out of turn, he understood, he would himself be sent to Number 76.

A guard took him upstairs to a room and told him to wait. When his father appeared, he was the first to break down. All in the space of a fortnight or so, my grandfather had been reduced to a shrunken wreckage. His wrists had raw red sores, from the rubbing of lacerating ropes or fetters. He tried to speak, but the words would not come and he stood there in silence, tears misting his eyes. You saw in those hollow eyes the hours, days, nights of torment endured – the shivers, vomitings, purgings, sweatings, and so on. He had undergone an exercise in gratuitous sadism, exquisite and prolonged. He had been through a cold turkey.

My father took his arm. He was gripped by an unaccustomed emotion: pity – my grandfather was not a person of whom one easily said, 'Poor man.' Very slowly they walked out together, down the steps of the front entrance to the waiting car. Later my grandfather would say, 'That was the very worst that ever happened to me.' That experience, more than any other, made him resolve to give up opium. After his release he resumed his habit, but with the hope that he might soon be broken of it. 'About time too,' Madame said. He felt he must give battle or sink; driven by the force of ghastly memories, he willed himself to abstinence.

The years ticked on, 1943, 1944, 1945. My parents were now married. To the war which you no longer saw, heard, or smelled, a numbing acclimatization had set in. It had become a stalemate, with the Japanese holding cities in the eastern half of China, and the Chinese government the vast tracts of the interior, the so-called Free China with its capital in Chungking. It wasn't peace exactly, but nor was it war. In Shanghai men and women still drank and danced with no brooding sense that they must savour their last and sweetest moments. Parties still stomped over polished floors to the sound of boogie-woogie. Of those who lived through that time, by no means all felt the ground sinking beneath their feet. My father, growing to manhood, floated through those years as through a time of reprieve, a period he was to remember, against all historical wisdom, as a golden age, daubed with high colour, coruscating with social scintillations – all signs of a disintegration he still did not see coming. That peculiarly Shanghainese freedom to press pleasure to intoxicated excess was good for another few years yet.

There was a time he went to classes at St John's on horseback, petrol was that hard to come by. But the black market changed things for the better. Horses he continued to keep, but for races and polo, not for getting about. How sweet it was, how delectably sweet, to hear the crowds roar their cheer as one of his stable, Feiteng ('soar'), named Freedom in English, finished first to take the silver cup at the Shanghai Recreation Club's first annual spring race meeting in 1943. Afterwards, flushed with triumph and pleasure, he ran beside it as Freedom cantered up Nanking Road, on the far side of the race track, cutting a dash in his silk-lined gown and his fashionable sunglasses. It was a moment nothing could undo. The soft May sun, the sweep of the now empty grandstands, the assuagement of the pain of all-out effort, the admiring glances – inside the ring of war, how beguiling was the cast which life could take. After she married him my mother started riding too, taking lessons from a Cossack, one of a large colony of Russians exiled by the Bolshevik revolution. How could they know that their generation was foredoomed?

Days like these, it was possible to believe the world outside would remain intact, that life would keep on much as before. People so easily grow used to the unusual. In the lake city of Hangzhou, where, one autumn, my parents took their first holiday together (and, had they but known it, their last in China), the rhythm of native life seemed undisturbed, regular as tides. There was space and a great stillness, the lake opening into the sky, and a sense of long days – years – to come. They rambled, fanned by a little breeze, in the sun and in shade, by the lake, through glades, and later on bridges above willow-reflecting water, and up the surrounding hills, now stopping to look down a rock pool, now for an exchange of pleasantries with a hill dweller, now in and out of a monastery, now pausing to read a poem engraved on weathered stone, then finding an inn and in it, the food of the country, a whole lake fish, Dragon Well tea in porcelain cups, a splash of warmed Shaoxing wine. The whole quite soothing, timeless; what right has war here, or intrusions of the future? Life is good, as good as it can ever be and – this can never end.

The inn was open in front, to let out the heat of the kitchen. Outside, the light was draining, and lanterns glowed faintly in the falling dusk. They ate in silence at first, enclosed by hubbub, then my father broke the pause with, 'It will not always be like this,' his eyes on his wife's young face, a moon in lamplight. He saw the girlish tousle to her hair, which that autumn she wore, unpinned, down to her shoulders, a cloud of natural curls, most unusual in a Chinese. She had on a light cashmere cardigan the colour of hay, and a pair of dark flannel trousers. All of a sudden an end-of-the-day feeling was upon him, a sense of the fragility of the world they had known; perhaps the powerlessness of all humanity to forestall or shield itself from loss.

It could scarcely be helped; but perhaps they could still help themselves. There was something to be said for simply getting out of Shanghai. My father saw his way: they would make for Free China, for Chungking. Chungking was the place Chiang Kai-shek had chosen for his exile; in Chungking you need have no truck with the Japanese.

He never thought to ask, What if I can't get through the blockade lines? You were sure to get through, because the front was pierced in three places. *Yin-yang* was how people described these equivocal places – not quite free, nor exactly occupied, points where people and goods (cotton, medicine, weapons, rubber tyres, food) moved back and forth without let or hindrance. Well might the Japanese soldiers look the other way, so great were the sums that changed hands. Was it, or was it not, smuggling? It was hard to say. Whatever it was, it brought Chinese and Japanese together in profitable collusion, and called thriving market towns into being where none had existed before. To one such town – Jieshou, at the junction of Anhui province and Henan – my father proposed to make his way. With Hanze he made arrangements for a caravan.

It was a party of six which set off from Shanghai: my parents, my mother's eldest brother and his wife, my mother's second sister Ming, and Hanze. They were laden with medicines, paper and tobacco – stuff they could sell in the interior. It seemed a long way from Shanghai to the hinterland, to the raggle-taggle villages of muddy cottages, to the blank peasant stares, to faces with no flicker of curiosity or interest in them, to whimpering children in rags, a good deal further than a couple of hundred miles – all the incalculable distance, in fact, between the modern world and the medieval.

The railroad came to an end at Bangbu, a town about two-thirds of the way to Jieshou. It seemed no more than a railway junction, busy, sleazy in parts, but this belied the sinister purposes served by Bangbu. The Japanese had long made it their business to fill the place with their agents – when it came to espionage, you could tell the Japanese little that they did not already know. Here they had solicited, of all things, the co-operation of the leaders and adherents of strange and secret mystical sects, reckoning in this way to win a following and foment trouble among the people, who were a superstitious lot, highly susceptible to religious persuasion and the mumbo-jumbo. One sect, disbanded by the local authorities, was particularly colourful, with self-styled adepts among the clergy, skilled at directing the flow of semen, up or down, by pressing on the right acupuncture points. That was Bangbu, the Shanghai arrivals were told, by those they tapped for local gossip.

At Bangbu they switched from rail to two-wheeled carts, hired from transport companies and pulled not by beasts of burden but by humans. It was almost high summer. The discomforts were staggering: the sun beating down, the dust, the filth, the uncertainty, the lack of amenities, the rutted road diminishing to treacherously pitted tracks. You could reach a point where your cart's every jolt had the impact of a jackhammer. The poverty of the countryside too, the sense of unremitting daily hardship, ground into them; they had never seen want on such a scale as this. By the time the carts drew up outside a hostelry, everyone would have had enough for the day, though hardly more than thirty-five miles would have been covered, so snail-like was the pace of the journey. Fearing fleas, the travellers would sleep on their own camp beds, three to a room, their eyes closing in weariness to the chorus of frogs and crickets. The sounds came through the door chinks and little windows of paper – these city slickers were among men who had yet to know glass. Their beds stood on floors of beaten earth, and they would wake to the gnawing of rats. The privies horrified the women: no flushing and the excrement of they didn't know how many days.

At last, the first lap completed, they arrived at Jieshou. This was the frontier, but it did not feel like life under the guns of the enemy. The place bristled with men bent on making what money they could while they could: profiteers such as could only be seen in a country at war. Every other man you met there seemed to be a dealer, or an agent for something. People came from the coast, from the inland regions, across the Yellow River and the Yangtze. The town was unbelievably prosperous, a long chalk from the indigent country they had just crossed. They planned on spending a few days here, seeing to arrangements for their onward journey, the hiring of transport for themselves and their goods and so on. But scarcely had they settled in their inn than my mother fell ill. Thinking of the wilds for which they were headed, and the hazards of the journey, everyone thought it best for her to go back to Shanghai. My father would take her, and then return to Jieshou. This was one of the few occasions in her life when my mother enjoyed the luxury of having things taken out of her hands.

The others were to travel ahead, to Chungking. But one cannot know from one day to the next what will happen in a war. It was as they were about to resume their journey that, with an extraordinary suddenness, the war ended. The bomb dropped on Hiroshima, on Nagasaki, the Japanese surrender on 14 August . . . a momentous turn of events which brought rejoicing people into the streets throughout the country.

They cheered at the news of victory in Chungking, how they cheered. With victory, every exile, every civil servant who had followed his government to Chungking, turned his thoughts to home . . . Shanghai, Nanking, Canton, Peking.

One moment you were bound for Free China; the next all

China was free. Suddenly all was confusion, with Chinese troops arriving to seize and disarm the Japanese garrisons, and refugees from occupied China making ready to leave for home. Hanze was to remember the time well. 'There we were, stuck in Jieshou, when everybody else was going home, clogging the roads, thronging the trains; and suddenly there was no market for the stuff we'd lugged all the way from Shanghai – all that cotton, tobacco, medicine simply went begging, when you'd have had people fighting for it not so long before. Oh, the shame of it!' The end of the war was the end of Jieshou as a profiteer's paradise.

What were they to do? The war was over, yet it would be too much to hope that this would mean the end of their worries. The Japanese had laid down their arms, but scarcely had they done so than civil war broke out. Victory had come, but not peace: there would be killing and dying in China for four long years yet. For good or ill the future of China would now hang on the outcome of another struggle – that between the Kuomintang and the communists.

Although there now seemed no point in going to Chungking, my aunts and uncle decided none the less to complete their journey, leaving Hanze to try and get rid of the goods in Jieshou. They travelled by two-wheeled carts, pulled by coolies, on tracks that wound through the deep country, circumventing the cities, and did at length arrive in Chungking, much the worse for wear. Hanze, meanwhile, despaired of offloading the goods in Jieshou. At some point he decided to give up on Jieshou and make instead for Xian, further into the interior. My grandfather had tendered for, and won, a government contract to build the waterworks in that town, and it would be as well to see how things were progressing. Besides, Hanze would not be alone in Xian: my grandfather had posted a foreman there, a fellow-Shanghainese on whose help and local contacts Hanze might be able to count.

There was also money in the bank, the millions of dollars my grandfather had remitted there for safe keeping, not foreseeing the dizzying inflation which would render them almost completely worthless.

That he would have no better luck in Xian was Hanze's first discovery. He was also dismayed to find that government officials had made free with the raw materials my grandfather had shipped there, the tons of steel, timber and cement the inland provinces lacked. The supplies never reached Xian, much less the construction site. The waterworks were never completed, nor was my grandfather ever paid. He was later to sue the government for breach of contract, but to no avail. Of course he should have known better, but then he had remained in Shanghai, and had not seen for himself how cynical, how rapacious, Chiang Kai-shek's government had grown in Chungking. It was in Xian that Hanze's eyes were opened to the corruption and dissolution of the nation.

Lunar New Year was approaching when Hanze was joined by my father – who, with the resumption of air services, had flown to Xian from Shanghai. The two agreed to try and shift the goods in Chengdu, further to the south-west. Why not? The stuff was not moving in Xian. When there is no choice one has to go on. They travelled with it as far as Baoji, where it was loaded on to trucks bound for Chengdu. It was in a dark drab inn in Baoji, so far from home, so unfamiliar and so without attractions, that they ate their New Year dinner together, cares crowding in, the civil war waging, the money dwindling. Baoji itself was no place for celebrations: it was dismal and bedraggled, with a misery unrelieved by any suggestion of the picturesque. Xian had at any rate what it had not – the interest of history; Xian had been an imperial capital, glorious in its time, whereas all Baoji was was a halt on the road to the far west.

The next day the two parted, my father to head back to Xian, Hanze to go on to Chengdu. All Hanze said, when he saw my father off, was, 'Remember me to the master.' Already, much could be left unsaid between them. His enquiries after my grandfather's health had drawn from my father the far from reassuring news that the master, as Hanze called him, was trying to give up opium. What was it that compelled him? Madame's insistence – could it be? She no doubt meant well, wanted him out of harm's way, yet her ruthlessness was appalling. Seeing how much it was costing him, my father had suggested that he and Madame went to live in Hong Kong for a bit. 'Hong Kong is British,' my father said; 'you can smoke in peace there.' He offered to take them. 'Give it a go. You might like it there, you can never tell unless you try.' The three of them made the journey. Much of the time Madame was edgy; things were not terrible but neither she nor my grandfather tried very hard to make themselves at home. Hong Kong *was* provincial, compared to Shanghai; they couldn't imagine anything happening here that could be important. Grandfather fretted, Madame sulked. Within a few weeks the boredom became insupportable. How best to make themselves understood, when they spoke next to no Cantonese, they never discovered. In no time at all they were back in Shanghai, and my grandfather continued to crave the solace of his pipe.

Is it true, the story told of Madame afterwards, that she flung his pipe on to the floor and broke it with the words, 'There, that'll stop you!', her voice cutting like a knife? There were many ready to think the worst of her. But what if there were? The fact remains that, wittingly or unwittingly, she was the one who nagged him into saying, 'I'll do it even if it kills me.'

'It did kill him,' Hanze later said; it might well have worn away what little resistance he had once possessed against heart failure.

When Hanze returned to Shanghai from Chengdu, after nearly eight months there, my grandfather had already taken to his bed.

'Master, I'm back,' Hanze said. He moistened a face towel and laid it on the forehead of the sick man. There was nobody else in the room.

'I've missed you.'

Hanze could tell, by the way he forced the words out, that my grandfather was past all help.

'Not all of the stuff went,' Hanze reported, 'but enough did.' It was the fear of shortage, renewed by the civil war, that had at last taken those wares off Hanze's hands.

The onset of evening was swift. Hanze sat quite still in the dark room. The two were alone, the master and the servant. Hanze sat for two days and two nights; and on the third, while my father and mother and Madame were at dinner, he saw my grandfather breathe his last. It was a January day in 1947, when my grandfather was in his fifty-sixth year.

8

A young man stood outside the gates of 116 Route Winling with his eyes on the doorman. He was in his early twenties, thin, with gentle apologetic eyes and thick eyebrows that resembled his father's. Young as he was, his shoulders were already hunched, as though bearing too much knowledge, imbibed too early, about the griefs and humiliation that lay in store. If he could, he would have rushed past the doorman and entered the house; he would have hurled himself, if he could, down by his father's deathbed. Two mornings had gone by, and two nights, and now, for the third day running, he was hanging about the cold street outside and wishing more than anything to be allowed inside the house.

But Afu, the doorman, knew there was no question of it. It wasn't as though Afu did not feel for the young man's situation, for he had a good heart, and believed past was past, but still orders were orders, and Madame had made it clear enough: open the door to the son of Jade Peach, and you may as well open the door to bad luck. Who was to question her when she said that she had had it foretold, that Yeshu's fate and my grandfather's were crossed, that the one would balefully clasp the other, throttling it to death? On no account must such a fate be allowed near the dying man, she had said, lest it hastened his death. You would have to range some larger reason than mere disbelief against such malevolence as hers.

The young man could see Afu looking away from him, not wanting to be tempted to some action he might later regret. Yet merely by standing there, waiting, he could make Afu relent. You could not say if it was Afu's oversight or his intention to leave the small side door unlatched when, without so much as looking round, he turned his back to buy a packet of cigarettes from a passing hawker. It was at that moment that Yeshu made a dash for the door. Up the front steps, into the door, across the front hall he strode, hurrying into a stumbling run up the stairs until further progress was blocked by two servants on the landing. Madame had said, hearing the approaching footsteps, 'Stop him, we cannot be too careful.' But he was past stopping, driven only to fling himself into his father's presence. He pushed the two servants aside, pulling off their hands on his arms, their protests weighing as nothing beside the urgency, the pathos, of his own need.

At last he was standing before his father, with whom people were taking turns and from whom everyone would soon be parted. With death already at the door, people had dropped into talking in lowered voices, and now there was simply silence. Madame was sitting at the bedside, and between Yeshu and her a charged look passed – defiance on his part, stony anger on hers. My father was there, and for the first time ever the two brothers looked into each other's eyes. My grandfather had waited to tell my father about Yeshu until the very last moment in which it was prudent or at any rate practical to do so.

Considering they had the same father, it is remarkable that their experiences should have been so different. It was not only that one grew up in Shanghai and one in Soochow, but that the one who grew up in Soochow should have lived a life of such penury. Because of the easy circumstances enjoyed by the one, the privations suffered by the other struck you the more; you marvelled at one son's patched jacket the more for the other son's Lagonda and race-horses. My father was brought up to believe that the world would arrange itself around him, and as he expected to find it, so, in a way, it became. By contrast his half-brother became early aware that he would never have his way without difficulty, and without strenuously defying his own circumstances. A habit of privilege made my father proof against any true sense of defeat, while no such advantage armoured the tender bruised pride of Yeshu.

How would it be if it had been Jade Peach who was promoted, from mistress to principal wife? Would she have set her son above my father, or would she have dealt justly between the two? The death of my grandmother set up a fateful crossroads, at which my grandfather could choose to further, or hamper, the cause of one son or the other. My father was the elder by eight months, but still Jade Peach might have seen to it that her son was first in all but name. Whether this would have weakened my father or whether it would have toughened him, sharpened the thrust of his ambition, I cannot quite say. Yeshu is the gentler creature, the sort to keep his head down; but with those years of pinch and pain behind him, can he be other than he is? A hard school can temper you, but it can cow you too.

That she should come off second-best stung Jade Peach to the quick, she who had felt herself first in my grandfather's affections. Playing second fiddle to Madame was quite out of the question, she could not think of it. She did hear someone say, 'Could she but swallow her pride, she would have remained his favourite, even while settling for less in the way of status'; but she knew it wasn't just a question of her pride, but of what Madame would do to her – she knew Madame would do her damnedest to exclude her, in order to fortify herself. An ugly squabble would have been certain; there would have been scene upon scene. It was as much to avoid these as out of pique that she stalked off to Soochow, taking her child with her.

Although she could not be entirely sure that my grandfather would come after her, bringing her his regrets to comfort, she was still devastated when weeks passed, and he did not appear. It was not then, but later, when she had given up all hope of a reunion, that she returned to Shanghai and brought a suit against him. What was at stake? Money, of course, but it was also more than money: it was the court's recognition of her claims as wife, and her son's rights as legitimate heir. Had she a case? One would have thought so. Yet it is not at all unusual for lawyers to wrest from judges triumphant verdicts for their clients even when these clients are patently and unmistakably in the wrong. To pay for such lawyers was well within my grandfather's means. Was there sleight of hand as well? There might well have been. To hear Niangniang tell it, the litigant's case fell by one piece of evidence – the fact that, in Soochow, the child was not known by my grandfather's name at all, but by that of another relative. The defence made much of this, pressing the case of questionable paternity way beyond its merits.

There were hours and days of talk, of conjectures over a word or look, tears, imprecations, shrill declarations before heaven and the gods. Emotions smouldered, and there was much nastiness all round – civility is the first casualty of a suit of this kind. One retrospective reading (Niangniang's) is that Jade Peach stood not a moment's chance. Why? Because justice is seldom done on behalf of the poorer and weaker portion of humanity? Because matters were determined not humanly, but legally?

Jade Peach, on hearing she was done for, instantly called down evil upon my grandfather and his descendants. Her imprecations were not taken seriously at the time, though there would be reason to be reminded of them two generations later. Of course she was paid off, but even so it was not an occasion for saying, 'No hard feelings.' Was it or was it not a generous sum with which they bought her silence? Nobody knows for sure, though Madame was heard to say, decades later, 'The money she got, the ungrateful wretch.' But then you could hardly take Madame's word for it. At all events, what money there was was soon dissipated; Jade Peach turned to the pipe, a costly habit. She remained in Shanghai, while her child was returned to Soochow, to be brought up in its outskirts by a relative of hers. Seven at the time, he was never to see his mother again. When the money for his keep – remitted regularly at first, then erratically – stopped coming altogether, it could only be assumed that he was abandoned. He found he had to fend for himself, not because the relatives with whom he lodged were especially heartless or ungenerous, but because it was all they could do to feed and clothe themselves and their own children.

So for all their dissimilarity of circumstance, he and my father had this in common, that in their different ways they were both motherless children.

Soochow lacked Shanghai's opportunities, one reason its loveliest women filled the singsong houses of the metropolis. You moved here for cheapness, for the reclusive tranquillity of its walled gardens, to get away from the hurly-burly of the city, to practise calligraphy perhaps, and to live the life of the retired scholar or poet-painter. Canals humped over by bridges, lanes of mellow paving, down-drooping weeping willows: these were all very well for the leisured seeker of quiet beauty, but the other side to them was that here time moved slowly, all but standing still or dawdling in some earlier era, uninvaded by change – and one's hour never arrived. Whereas a boy of twelve or thirteen might live by his wits and dream of striking it rich in Shanghai, here, in this small town of bounded horizons, he could not will himself up any rung, social or economic.

Here the abandoned boy lived chancily, on the crumbs of a far from ample table. His lot was not made easier by the outbreak of war, which added a colouring of embattlement to the skimpiness of life in Soochow. His only consolation was that he was a star pupil, much praised by his schoolteachers. The school fees he paid himself, with money earned copying sutras for a nearby Buddhist temple. He copied the sutras on to rolls of red paper, with a brush soaked in gold ink. The monks supplied the paper and ink and paid him a fee for his labours; the inscriptions were sold to pilgrims during their devotional visits to the monastery. He was fourteen or fifteen at the time, but his calligraphy had already an elegant adult assurance, the strokes disciplined and fluid, each character immaculately executed. Even today, one looks at his handwriting and thinks, Such script as this could only have evolved through ceaseless practice.

It was a pittance, what he earned, and he might never have owned a cotton gown had a sympathetic class teacher not given him one as a present. To make it wear longer, he would take the gown off and hang it up the moment he came home from his classes. That same teacher helped get him a job when he left school, as an admissions clerk at a charity hospital. With such savings as he had, he went on weekend expeditions to Shanghai, where he scoured every street he could remember having walked as a child for signs of his father and mother.

One day in 1941, quite by chance, he bumped into a man he recognized from his early childhood in Shanghai: a close friend of his mother's, who he knew was acquainted with his father as well. 'Uncle Chen,' he called out in surprised delight as he went forward to introduce himself; here was somebody who could lead him to his parents. But delight turned instantly to disappointment when Uncle Chen said no, he was no longer in touch with Jade Peach; and as for Yeshu's father, they hadn't seen each other for a very long time. 'Here's some money,' said Uncle Chen, who could tell from the account the boy gave of himself that things were far from dandy. He was put out when the boy turned it down, imploring only that he lead him to his father. Uncle Chen undertook to help the boy with an earnestness that might, or might not, have been genuine.

Six months passed. An emissary arrived with fifty silver dollars, a fortune at the time. 'Buy yourself some clothes,' he said to Yeshu. 'You have to look presentable when you go to meet your dad.'

'When?'

'Well, not just yet. But you'll hear from your father in due course, I promise.'

But Yeshu was not to be fobbed off with empty promises, and a good deal of sweet talking was necessary to cajole him out of his determination to tag along when the man made to return to Shanghai. The man had been wrong to think he could disengage himself from Yeshu quickly.

After he left Yeshu resumed his own quest in Shanghai, searching all the more thoroughly for having the fifty dollars for fares and the rooming house. To no avail, it proved – those he asked said, 'We don't know,' meaning they would not say; and in any event his father had moved, unbeknown to him, from Avenue Foch to Route Winling.

It was another half-year before the emissary reappeared. This time he could afford to be less cagey; he had instructions for a donation of two hundred silver dollars to be given to the hospital and for Yeshu to be brought back to Shanghai.

But not to his father, not straight away. Lodgings were provided in a house near the Bridge of the Eight Immortals (in fact the room where Hanze lives today), and a guardian in the form of Madame's eldest sister, a singsong girl by profession. For a reunion with his father, prospects seemed no brighter. Instead, there was a renewal of acquaintance with the world of the singsong house, which he abhorred. That Madame was the one who baulked him of his wish was not known till later, nor how great her hold had become over his father, whose opium habit weakened his ability to assert himself.

There was nothing Yeshu could do about any of it, unless – unless, a soft-hearted observer came forward to suggest, he flung himself in front of his father's car as it headed up into Avenue Pétain. This person was a frequent caller at 116 Route Winling, familiar with the household's daily round – which days of the week my grandfather took the car out to be about his business, at what hour he started on his expeditions, and so on.

And that was how it came about that a chauffeur found his way barred one morning by a youth with upraised arms not far from the intersection with Avenue Pétain, and a son made himself known to a father not seen for eleven and more years through a window with the pane wound down.

Great as it was, the change, within a single day, from rejection to acceptance would have been greater still had Yeshu been allowed to live in 116 Route Winling; yet it would have been surprising if Madame had agreed to it. He moved instead to quarters on the premises of the leather factory, and in time passed the entrance exams to a not undistinguished university.

It could not but be Madame who had ordered, when the mourning garments were distributed, that Yeshu be given only a white sash to wear. Had he not protested, not only would he not have worn the gown of white ramie befitting a bereaved son, but even the servants would have looked in deeper mourning. In such ways was his inferior status cruelly and repeatedly brought home to him. It was only his insistence that secured him the proper clothing.

The casket, of solid yellow cedar full five inches in thickness, had a locking device, worked by driving wooden stoppers into a series of holes in the lid. My father had been standing still by the casket, but when the stoppers were being hammered into the lid, he bent forward to rub the surface with his hands, as one would one's muscles to lessen the pain of an injury. He rubbed hard, as a masseur might, and as good form required. And as if to drown out the noise of the pounding mallet, the trumpeters rose from their seats to blow loudly on their instruments.

I write this description of my grandfather's funeral from what I remember of the account my mother gave of it; Hanze was the one who supplied the rest of the story. In the ordinary course of events my grandfather's body would have been shipped to his native village and buried there, but civil war and my father's departure for Hong Kong followed by the communist victory interfered with this plan and, after it had lain for four years in the Chusan Guild, the coffin was eventually interred in Shanghai.

Hanze made for the cemetery as soon as he got back from serving his sentence in labour camp, only to find it had vanished – the tombs flattened, the headstones pressed into service as paving and pillars. His enquiries revealed that my grandfather's coffin had been saved in the nick of time; Madame had had it exhumed and transported to her native Soochow, the place where she made her last home and where, with a remittance from my father, a plot was bought in the Lingya Cemetery. In retrospect one realizes that she need hardly have gone to all that trouble, since there would be no escaping the Red Guards when the Cultural Revolution erupted; these would make short work of lives in their prime, let alone graves.

As for Madame herself, she was ruined and died embittered. You would scarcely have credited it at the time of her husband's death; at that time you imagined her *en route* from a comfortable middle age (she was forty-eight or -nine at the time) to a well-cushioned old age. To her my grandfather had, five years before he died, made over the ownership of 116 Route Winling; and in his will he had supplemented this gift with a number of bequests, including substantial shares in the leather factory. All this, when revealed, was a shock to my father, who never saw himself as anything other than first heir. For a concubine to inherit was unusual enough; for her to do so at the expense of the first wife's son was unthinkable. My father counted himself as good as dispossessed. From decency more than choice, he didn't accuse her of having exercised undue influence on his father, though that was certainly what he thought. And he suspected her of falsity when she said, feeling something owing, 'It'll all be yours when I'm gone,' because if there was one cause she promoted above all others, it was that of her own Di family. Besides, shrewd as she was in some matters, she was foolish and gullible when it came to others, and there would be no shortage of expectant hangers-on to cheat her out of her money.

At around the time of the revolution she converted overnight from Buddhism to Christianity, causing more stir among her Di relatives than might reasonably be occasioned by an event of this kind because it was seen to have been inspired by a preacher, a man much given to shedding on his flock smiles partly knowing and partly ingratiating, on whom she fell into the habit of pressing handsome donations. If these relatives of hers supposed her to be a dupe of this preacher, the fact that he never seemed in any hurry to leave when he visited her at her home did nothing to

make them change their minds. Come to that, they found
themselves wondering (having not until now been exposed to
this religion), was it standard practice for the preacher to call so
frequently at the home of a member of his congregation?

Yet she was never anything but generous when it came to her
Di relatives, and no sooner did my mother leave Shanghai to join
my father in Hong Kong than the house filled with Madame's
nephews and nieces. She made my sister, brother and me vacate
our rooms and sleep with Nanny Moon in what used to be the
dining room – a move that proved prelude to our being turfed
out of the house altogether. Nanny Moon, who had provided
Madame with her excuse – they had had words – found us rooms
in a building ill-sited by the standards of 116 but still in a
desirable neighbourhood of the French Concession, and moved
us in with Hanze's help. We did not stay there long before we,
too, left Shanghai for good.

Those were eventful times, times when from one day to the
next there was no knowing what misfortune might not befall
one. Shortly after lunch one November day in 1952, Madame
received a notice from the People's Criminal Court of Shanghai
informing her that her late husband had been found guilty of high
treason – he had 'given assistance to the Japanese and hurt the
cause of national resistance' – and all his assets were to be treated
as enemy property and confiscated forthwith by the state. She
was to lose her house.

'But it is my one means of support,' she protested in an appeal
which she got a lawyer to draft for her. 'I am a poor woman,' she
pleaded, 'old and widowed, without children to care for me.
Surely the court (with due respect) would bring Chairman Mao
Zedong's precept to bear on this case?' – she meant, and spelled
out, the one about dealing 'leniently with the past, firmly with
the present'. To show herself much put upon, she even brought

my father in, saying he'd contrived to do her out of her due, and might have succeeded had she not had it out with him. One straw she pounced upon was the fact that possession of the property had passed to her years before her husband's death – and doesn't the new marriage law, she asked, recognize that wives, too, have legal title to property, so that, 'Even if my husband's assets were to be confiscated, might not this house, his gift to me, be spared?'

And in case the suppliant approach didn't work, she challenged the court's finding, setting out reasons why my grandfather could not be termed a collaborator. She sent separate letters to the People's Committee for Investigation and the East China Committee for Military Affairs, it having not yet come home to her that for these champions of the unpropertied classes, expropriation was a good occasion for plunder. Where were the high-ups of the new régime to live if not in the villas and apartments of the supplanted bourgeoisie?

Though her appeal was vouchsafed a hearing three and a half months later, she became one of those people found waiting anxiously on benches in this or that government office eight, nine, ten months after their cases had opened. Seeing the woman who left at last for Soochow, you might have felt towards her an entirely new sentiment: compassion.

Worse still was to come. A distant relative persuaded her to part with a good deal of her savings – 'a business venture that will double your money', was the way he put it to her, either over-optimistically or duplicitously. Then, in the course of a particularly virulent political campaign, the state made her repay the money she had received for disposing of her share of the tannery. Her money thus eroded, she lived by selling her jewellery, bit by bit, until there was none left. She was impoverished, lonely, and not a great age, sixty-two, when she died. 'She drank herself to death,' I was told by a niece of hers whom Hanze helped to track down in Shanghai. 'It was a couple of bottles of *wujiapi* a day,' she said, naming the millet spirit which Madame gulped, on the rocks, to drug herself into insensibility.

Niangniang's words, when she heard the story, were, 'Well, things catch up with you,' a comment to which she appended, with that half-shake of the head with which she signals a foregone conclusion, the Buddhist explanation for everything: karma.

9

Shanghai's fall to communism was only two years off. My parents
had lost their Lagonda, but they were still eating their meals off a
dinner service bearing their own family hallmark, fine *wucai*
porcelain ordered from the famous kilns of Jingdezhen; waited
on by servants commanded by a bark or murmur or meaningful
glance. They went dancing still, *soignés* in their furs and satins,
even though the giddy inflation was devaluing the *yuan* in their
pockets fivefold, tenfold, thirtyfold . . . and what bought a
twelve-course banquet last week and a chicken yesterday would
barely run to an egg this evening. Half the world had altered, it
was time to draw in your horns, but still they kept a glow on life,
as people will on the day before Judgement Day, sipping nectar
from poisonous flowers.

They hardly knew what to think any more. One year it was
everybody saying, 'Let's have done with civil war.' The next it
was hostilities as usual. For all the talk of a negotiated peace, the
Kuomintang and the communists were still at each other's
throats. How would it all end? Not so long before, a communist
victory was the last thing in anyone's mind. Now you couldn't be
sure. Would no one appear at the eleventh hour offering rescue?
They heard it said that American succour was half-hearted, yet

they could scarcely credit this, habituated to the idea of the US in the role of *deus ex machina*. Nothing had seemed beyond the reach of American power and generosity at the time of the great victory over the Japanese; and to the imagination of a battered and exhausted city, the arrival of American GIs in Shanghai had seemed like a promise of great times ahead. With that eternally hopeful air of theirs, that aura of limitless bounty, Americans so easily inspired optimism. Peace could, once again, be the making of Shanghai, which in that moment of grace had felt the best of all places to be, buoyed, renewed, its fate no longer equivocal.

No question about it, the Americans *were* what everyone called them when they first came to town: *dinghao*, the 'very best'. Their presence was essential to that ambiance of victory, the cheering in the streets, the imagined sensation of being showered with confetti.

Only, they liked to be on the side of the angels, these Americans, to have all things both ways; to have their cake and eat it, to extricate themselves from the embrace of Chiang Kai-shek but not to fall into the arms of Mao Zedong, to be doctrinally antipathic to communism yet avowedly idealistic. If only the Kuomintang could have had the communists' puritanical fervour and self-discipline, they thought, without the Marxism. It was a pity you couldn't have a better object for your philanthropy: unreliable, predatory, corrupt, the Kuomintang government did not come up to snuff. It was not the sort of government to which even Americans would say, If you need anything, you need only tell us. Yet many, far too many, were the people who held on to the hope that US dollars might miraculously halt the advance of the enemy.

My parents were two such people. Until it looked them in the face, they never dreamed it would be all up with the Kuomintang. If they knew what was good for them, they would be packing their bags. Yet who would have thought that the euphoria of '45 would subside so quickly? No doubt there were onlookers who saw the writing on the wall, but my parents were not among them; they could not have been less prepared. (That's what comes perhaps of having been brought up to money and to the sweetness of life.) But now they noted the calamitous rush of events and marvelled at their own innocence of two or three years ago. So incurious, so immersed in the moment, they seemed to have been in that state of euphoria which so often accompanies the dying: death's precursor. When, years later, my mother's mind went back to the old times, the good times, she would say: 'Think of it, the insouciance, the gaiety, the comfortable certainty that was such a far cry from what one felt later.' There was that gala night in which she waltzed with General Joseph W. Stilwell, commander-in-chief of the China-Burma-India theatre and chief of staff to Chiang Kai-shek – her long step gliding sideways, in tune with his, into the pools of floor that cleared for them. How festive it was; how splendid the men with their coat-tails twirling; how gorgeous the women with their brilliant painted faces and their sandalwood fans wafting to and fro, light as moths above the shadows. It never occurred to her to ask, How can it last? She was young, just young.

Later the uncle who had got her the invitation to the ball – he was something high up in the central government – was heard to remark on the recall of General Stilwell and his replacement by General Albert Wedemeyer. He did not say so, but there was bad, very bad, blood between Chiang Kai-shek and Joseph Stilwell. The two were worlds apart, the Chinese autocrat and the American liberal. This was well known; but what was not so well known was that Stilwell was only one of a steady stream of Americans to discover that they had had enough of Chiang Kai-shek. As for Wedemeyer, such was the mood of frivolity, of innocence, that he was famous not so much for what he did in the war as for what he did for Shanghai fashion – he gave his name to the Wedemeyer Jacket, as it was called by the trendsetters, the last word in casual wear.

One might say, the same old story: the nonchalance and the frivolity followed by the rude awakening; the sudden discovery that the enemy is at the gates, the battle is as good as lost, you are already on the brink of ruin.

On my father, the change was sprung in a particularly menacing way. One day, at the tannery, he found himself set upon by his employees, militant in their demand for a wage increase. He heard them say, their faces hard and cold with insistence, 'If you think you're going to be home in time for supper then you are very much mistaken.' He was incredulous, then indignant; everybody was feeling the pinch, nobody was having an easy time of it; he tried to reason with the labour leaders but found himself harangued and manhandled. They pressed close about him, they pinioned his arms and yelled at him. This went on all evening and well into the night. Then they thrust him into a windowless room and locked it, leaving him there in the dark, dazed and dishevelled, slumped in a chair.

He was a prisoner counting the hours to the time of his release. How long, how unbearably long are the hours when one wishes them past with no end in view; when one doesn't know how any of it will end, if it will ever end. What else could he do but to wait for the break of day, when someone, Hanze perhaps, would come looking for him?

Sleepless in the early hours, he had all the time for reflection; he could not stop thinking, What now? He was not thinking of what might transpire the next day or the day after, but what turn his whole life might now take, what cataclysmic change might now be forced upon the world that he had known. For he saw the threat to his existence, a threat of which his assailants were at once the portents and the instruments. He discerned the hand of the communists in what happened that day in the factory; for without the communists egging them on, these workers should hardly have been so inflamed or truculent. The communist underground had been infiltrating and organizing Shanghai's labour unions for years, and now, with skyrocketing prices and lay-offs making life daily, hourly, more difficult for the worker, its hour had struck. When economics go awry, politics do not loiter far behind.

Discerning communism's advance in the hum of ever-deepening public disgruntlement, in strikes staged by workers and in rallies called by students, the Kuomintang government did what came naturally to it – sudden arrests by the secret police, assassinations, mysterious disappearances, the gagging of the press. To put down a strike at the beginning of the year, tanks had been used. Espionage and tale-bearing went from bad to worse, and any suspected liberal walked in danger. An uncle of my mother's was a casualty; he who called himself a patriot was murdered one night by agents of the central government, smothered to death with a pillow stuffed with goose feathers, in his own room, only minutes after he became aware of the two strangers who reared out of the shadows.

Yet it was obvious to any impartial observer that the central government was slipping down a steeply inclined plane, at the bottom of which lay only bankruptcy. It would take more than even tanks now to deal with the communists. No city, town or village was without its communist sympathizers, Party men of the underground. More and more now were the people who staked their lives on the communist creed, the only philosophy they had for going on with the grim job of living.

By the time Hanze came for him, shortly after sun-up, my father's mind was made up. He would leave Shanghai, with whose doom he would not wish his fate to be mingled. He knew Hong Kong a little and could think with equanimity about setting up there. Once settled, he would come back for his family. 'It's for the best,' he said to his wife. To Hanze he said, 'I'll send for you first, within the month; I'll need you there.'

Hanze was silent, but his gaze said, I'll go wherever you are.

His wife saw him off, a child in her arms. They came down the steps from the house and crossed the courtyard to the front entrance. A motor cycle stood by the gates, the motor cycle he was taking to the dealer to whom he had already made over the Buick and the Lagonda; he was stopping at the dealer's on his way to Hongqiao Airport, and taking a taxi for the rest of the journey. For a few seconds they stood facing each other by the gates, then he got on the bike without speaking – he could think of no words that were not meagre. Only when the engine started did he reassure her, 'I'll come for you as soon as I can.'

She seemed utterly composed, staring straight before her. As he drove down Route Winling her eyes followed him. Then, as if to go after him and to call him back, she started to run down the road. Perhaps the weight of the child in her arms made her unsteady on her feet, or perhaps she stumbled over a bump in the asphalt, but just as she saw him approach the turn-off for Route Destelan, she pitched forward and, heeling sideways, fell hard on the pavement. She scrambled up, horror creeping over her, only dispelled when she saw that the baby was unhurt, only a little dirty and grazed on the cheek. On her feet again, she became aware that she herself was draggled with blood; she thought it had run from her forehead, but she couldn't be sure. Painfully, she made for the house, and all at once her mind steadied and the full force of her husband's departure struck home.

He never came back to Shanghai. With startling suddenness Manchuria fell to the communists within a month of his departure, on the last day of October 1948. In January 1949, in the full tide of their victories, communist troops entered Peking. Now for the sweep to the Yangtze, to open the way south to Nanking, Shanghai, and the rest of China. It was a Wednesday morning, 25 May, after token resistance by Kuomintang troops, that soldiers of the People's Liberation Army were spotted in the streets of Shanghai and white flags were glimpsed on buildings. At the Capitol they were showing *Hamlet*, with Laurence Olivier; and at the Grand, *I Wonder Who's Kissing Her Now*.

To leave or not to leave: everywhere there was talk of this, of whether the communists were the very devil or a change for the better. Those who spoke of departure and starting life anew in Hong Kong or America spoke in hushed voices – hushed because departure was at once like betrayal and surrender. Yet by no means everyone was seized by the impulse of flight. We have lived through so much, many shrugged; the worst has happened so many times; can anything appear to us as new in life, can anything appear as a surprise? If they were businessmen they thought they might strike a bargain with the new masters – what didn't they know about striking bargains? They'd done this successfully enough with the Kuomintang, with the Japanese even; why shouldn't they be able to do the same with the communists? If you tried to argue that the communists were different, none of them wanted to know, none had time for any more than the reinforcement of preconceptions. How can they be different? Less corrupt, yes; unbribable, no. No reason why you shouldn't do business with them. (Nothing causes so much blindness as the wish to believe.)

Hardly had the People's Government imposed itself than the out-and-out careerist was thinking, I'll bet on this horse, it'll carry me far. If it pushes people down, it raises them too. The number of public officials will increase fivefold, tenfold; I'll have a bright future ahead of me. How was this opportunist to know that there was little room at the top, that those up there would for the most part stay up there, and the wrangling would get worse with family trees and time-honoured privileges done away with? That whoever wants power will have to fight for it with everything he's got, tooth and nail and cunning, since he who has it will never give it up?

It would be a régime under which it would always be to someone's interest that someone else should be unseated. And that was scarcely the half of it. Everything private would enter the public domain. For the state to own schools and factories should not hurt one, but state newspapers, state books, state bed linen, state mothballs, state shoes, state cabbages, state tooth-brushes, state zip fasteners, state haircuts are another matter. In time, even your opinions and conscience would come to be state-owned.

Yet many were the capitalists who stayed on in Shanghai because they couldn't bear to part with their properties or jettison their investments, or because they had come to feel that they could live nowhere else. For not realizing that a person could lose something worse, they would pay dear. A hand would be felt on their arm, and an official voice heard to say: 'Come with us.'

All of my mother's family were stayers-on: her parents, her brothers and sisters. None of my father's were. I have often wondered about this: why had my father not cared to chance his luck under the new régime? None of his contemporaries knew very well what was to become of them, but whereas many of them were prepared to give communism the benefit of the doubt, he never saw it as anything other than a blight. He seemed to have taken its measure; he knew it to be the ruin of lives and dreams. Perhaps his dispossession by Madame provided added reason for leaving; were it not for that, there might have been more to miss. There could also be this to it, that while others lived with their minds clenched against the next assault of the unfamiliar, he had it in him, at a time when people spent their entire lifetime in one place, to rise to the challenge of dislocation; he had the get-up-and-go of the emigrant. He was a gambler, not a man to wait on events. His being a parvenu must have been part of it: that energy needed to claim a place for oneself had not yet been bred out of him; it had not atrophied, as it had in my mother's family, which comes from a long lineage, assured for generations of its stake and standing in society. To be gently born can be disabling. He, on the other hand, was anything but a flabby sybarite, incapable of struggle. His roots in Shanghai were the more easily torn up for being comparatively shallow. He was not locked in his time or place, not the kind to be left behind while elsewhere history swept on.

The place, though, would persist in his memory, faded, as even the most intense dreams fade; only two or three people standing out in diamond sharpness, the thought of whom stirred sorrow too deep to permit questioning.

He did send for Hanze, who was with him when he took his seat on the Hong Kong Stock and Gold Exchange, and saw his company Yuan Yuan go from strength to strength. My mother flew to join them, only to return to Shanghai in 1952 to see to the liquidation of such assets as still remained. She was accompanied by Hanze, who would know the accounting side of the matter better than anyone; the Bamboo Curtain had yet to come down for good and one moved fairly freely between Hong Kong and Shanghai. She sold what she could. It didn't amount to much but it was something. She then left again for Hong Kong. I don't remember saying goodbye to her; she left hurriedly, perhaps to have leaving over. Why she didn't take her children with her was not explained to us at the time; nor, at that age, would we have understood. Hanze escorted her as far as Canton, where she took leave of him at the railway station and changed from train to aeroplane. This was after she had been put through a probing customs inspection and a body search by two sexlessly uniformed women apparently chosen for their compulsion to leave no stone unturned. To rip out the lining and shoulder pads of her leopardskin coat had given these two evident satisfaction. Gold had not been found, only a diamond ring sewn into a sleeve. They allowed her to keep it. Not one to think tolerantly of her enemies, my mother had surmised that had there been two pieces of jewellery to confiscate, her inspectors would have pocketed them, one each.

In Shanghai, all day, my siblings and I either loafed or played. 'School,' my mother had said, 'is quite out of the question, you'll only get brainwashed.' Whereas Miss Shen, well educated, willing, was just the thing for us. Our governess was young, fragile, soft-voiced, from a well-to-do family but with prospects of an agreeable marriage dimmed by an otherwise beautiful face tragically scarred by smallpox. She had an apologetic manner and was easily embarrassed. Had I been older, her timidity would have prompted an effort of reassurance in me, but just then I had the callousness of children. My ignorance was the handicap left by my zeal to discomfort her. She didn't last long. There had been attempts at lessons, but we couldn't have learned anything: when I began school in Hong Kong some years later, my mother was horrified to discover that I could neither read nor write.

What I did learn I must have picked up in the alleys. In the schools they were singing:

The east is red,
The sun is up.
China has brought forth a Mao Zedong.
How hard he toils for the people.
Heigh-ho: he is our great saviour.

But we preferred the other version, sung in innocent disrespect by all the neighbourhood children:

The east is red,
The sun is up.
Mama gets up to empty the commode.
The commode falls into the river.
Heigh-ho: she fishes out a Mao Zedong.

All this must have been before the terror. The People's Government had begun by being fairly gentle: the lull before the storm. The turn for the worse occurred at about the time of the Korean War, though between the two circumstances there was not necessarily a causal relation: it did not need a mood of embattlement for the Communist Party to show its colours; it would have done so sooner or later, war or no war. The military threat might have accounted for the exigence but not for the showing itself.

In those days one never was out of the reach of a siren or public loudspeaker, or a wall daubed with exhortatory slogans. With the war, American venality was given saturation publicity. I didn't know it, of course, for the propaganda it was. I merely noted the cartoons of American tanks retreating before Chinese soldiers with fixed bayonets; of Korean babies machine-gunned by US troops; and of puny figures, understood to be English, licking the boots of an unshaven, green-faced MacArthur. At anti-US rallies, a Chinese would be got up in a frock coat, a red-and-white-striped top hat and a long false nose, and led through the crowds to be jeered at. But what I liked best were the parades, rivers of people bearing giant portraits of a goateed Lenin, a bemedalled Stalin, and a cloth-capped Mao Zedong, wart and all.

The war was the thing that had intervened between my mother's first departure from Shanghai and her second. That and my father's bankruptcy. To say that the war had nothing to do with the failure of my father's business in Hong Kong would be to deny the rush buying of gold prompted by the outbreak of hostilities and the temptation this created for speculators to overreach themselves, though it was never this circumstance that my father would blame, but his own inexperience. He might also have put it down to the hand of Fate, being not so much Buddhist as fatalistic. Ordained or not, the blow to his pride was severe, and he would cross the street to avoid coming face to face with a fair-weather friend.

He and my mother had given up their apartment on Robinson Road and moved to a hotel in Kowloon. What a demoralizing time that was; the awful blankness of it, when one day of forced idleness passed and another just like it began, when to roam the streets gazing into shop windows was the sum of one's evening diversion. They were eaten up with worry. They literally didn't know where their next meal would come from; they who had scorned freeloaders as beneath contempt were frequently reduced – the humiliation of it – to cadging meals off Great-uncle Zulai, who had escaped to Hong Kong with Danu and was ensconced in a flat in Causeway Bay. Zulai was the sort to have something up his sleeve no matter what happened. Mysteriously in funds, he made them welcome enough, but they stopped dropping in when

Danu said, once too often, 'Oh, here you are again – what perfect timing. Trust you two to turn up just as dinner is starting.'

Not even a roof could my father ensure his children, if they were to join him in Hong Kong. In Shanghai, between the house on Route Winling and the grandparents in Carter Road, a life could at least be contrived. Better to leave them there – what other possibility could he envisage? Homeless, lacking any confidence in the future, he could make no plans for the resumption of his ordinary family life or look further than the immediate present. He was at the end of his tether; leaving us in Shanghai seemed to him the only way out.

But more than a way out, he had to think of a way on. Malaya was to be that, though at the time it had seemed more like *terra incognita*. The DC3 bound for the unknown was boarded on Christmas Day, 1952. I have a letter from him written on a Concorde flight to New York in which he says that he could never embark on a long air journey without experiencing afresh the wretchedness of that day twenty-eight years ago. In Malaya lay the chance to make or break – which would it be? As he stared out of the window, all that he could find to console himself with was the thought that anything was preferable to life behind the Iron Curtain.

In Malaya he cast about for something to do and sought a start in rubber plantations. His being able to play bridge and polo rendered him acceptable to the British managers of the Standard Chartered Bank and the Hongkong and Shanghai Bank, and loans were secured. Enough Malay was learned; men were hired. It all took time and immense amounts of energy. He contended with the tropical heat and got on with it. When he had a shower each night after work, he'd leave a scab of silt in the tub, slough of his day's labours in the grit of a world yet to be made. To the home he contrived in the country that Chance assigned him, his family eventually came. Seeing him for the first time in years as he came up the pier to meet us off our boat, I was half embarrassed to greet him, not knowing him for my father, so black was he from the sun.

10

I think I remember the early years of People's Shanghai, but memory is so biased, so subject to rearrangement and shifts of angle, bringing to life only what it chooses, distorting events to give your past the particular significance you want it endowed with. You think you remember, but no doubt you have mixed in scraps from all sorts of later renderings, by your contemporaries, even from your own. Do you really remember hearing that, or do you remember being told you heard it? Did it happen *then*, at one time, or is the scene you remember a palimpsest, the sum of many others slurred into one?

I see the lawn, the bushes, the trees; it is the French Park, where I am taken to play of a morning or afternoon – or some other garden? I see Nanny Moon treading heavily into the green shades, her feet not as deformed as they might have been, not the 'golden lilies' that, but for the footbinder's half-heartedness and Nanny Moon's screams, they should have become. I see two children – or three? I feel the air, which is neither warm nor cold, and seems to belong to no season. The park is empty; this could seem strange, to anyone who stops to think about it. Something or other is afoot, even from far off one feels it. In a minute, there will be heard the filtered rumble of lorries. Dying out, this noise will give way to the sounds of human activity – of what activity particularly it will be impossible to tell. Then a long hush; and in this quiet shots will ring out, a volley of bullets from a firing squad.

I relive this moment more than thirty years later, when I meet a Party apparatchik who, for a wonder, listens to my questions and answers them honestly. I would have preferred that the gunfire had been my private hallucination, but no, he says, people *were* executed wholesale. Who? So-called counter-revolutionaries. How many? Truckloads. Thousands. Countless numbers sinking to their knees to be annihilated in an instant by the executioner's bullet, after paying for which the relatives were allowed to remove the body. Where? Oh, all over; in the outskirts mostly, but downtown too, when the numbers piled up and they had to rush them through.

Not the French Park? Yes, there too.

It is beyond me to ask, How do you know, were you there? He looks, of all things, ashamed, this man whose heart once beat for the Party and who raised clenched fists at those of my class and shouted, 'Death to the bourgeoisie!' I imagine him a child-faced soldier, fresh from the farms, dirt-poor; believing himself to be in a world made good, taking the Party's word for it; doing in 'bourgeois vermin' for the sake of a better tomorrow, little suspecting that tomorrow can be indefinitely adjourned, leaving him yearning, thirty-five years on, for fifteen square metres of living space yet knowing he can never have more than what he has.

He mumbles: 'It was campaign-time.' This by way of explanation or self-exoneration.

He means the time when there was no knowing at whose door the Black Marias might draw up next; and when what began as hearsay or a word in the ear could culminate in ruin or the executioner's bullet, or both, with suicide as a possible means of escape, all too frequently resorted to.

A time of terror, lying about inside my head like a fragmented picture, to assemble which is impossible, too many of the pieces are broken or missing; but of which I can reconstitute two or three moments, unclouded still, but all out of order.

One: my little brother on Nanny Moon's lap, the four of us squeezed into a pedicab. We are being pedalled down Nanking Road. So much meets my eye as we trundle along – flashes of colour from shop windows, from vendors' corners. There are cars on the road, but no rickshaws – these having been banned by the new government as being retrograde and degrading, savouring of bourgeois exploitation. I am leaning forward, the better to see the passing scene, when suddenly the driver pulls to a stop, mutters something to Nanny, and jerks down the tarpaulin curtains of the pedicab, at once blotting out our view.

'But it isn't raining,' I protest to Nanny. Hard to imagine there'd be a downpour to rebound from the lowered tarpaulin, with the sky clear, the sun out.

She has the grim look she wears whenever she tries to pour cod-liver oil between my pursed lips. 'No, but we're passing something not fit for your eyes.'

Whatever can that be? I am not told by Nanny, nor by anyone that I can remember; yet I seem to know, even then, and not just later, that a man has just jumped out of a window. A suicide leap. There were many, that spring. They chose Nanking Road for the tallness of its buildings. The one thing wrong with it was the crowdedness of its pavements; it was not easy to avoid the swarms of pedestrians below, and a number of passers-by were injured or crushed to death by the falling bodies.

For the rest of that spring, our trips down Nanking Road would never be in anything other than a blacked-out pedicab, rain or shine. You didn't know what you might be catching sight of, you couldn't say what you might not be bumping up against.

Close to that memory of suicide comes another. It belongs to a night I spent in the Lee house in Carter Road. Visiting our Lee grandparents was a treat, eagerly looked forward to by us children. There was always so much going on in that house. So many callers would arrive on one errand or another; if it wasn't the tailor, it would be the chiropodist, or else it was famous house-guests like Zhang Daqian, the great classical painter. There were always paintings about the house, sent by art dealers on approval to Grandfather Lee, who had an excellent eye, and a collection bearing many colophons from the eleventh and twelfth centuries. (The whole of which – the scrolls, the rare editions, the seals – was to vanish, following a swoop by rampaging Red Guards in 1966.) There was something so reassuring about the life in that house, the bustle in its corridors, the cooking stoves heating up day and night, the salvers of sweets and candied fruits handed around, that I always felt better – safer somehow, more proof against harm – for having gone there.

So I was the more taken aback when, in the night of my visit, I was wakened in the small hours by a sound so unmistakable yet improbable that for a moment I lay puzzling, until the matter was settled by voices on the outside landing. I hadn't dreamed it: a revolver *had* gone off downstairs; I caught enough of the babble outside my door to know that a man had pointed one to his head and blown his brains out.

Not long after the communist takeover, the house in Carter Road suffered the fate that routinely befalls dwellings in people's republics: the transformation of private residences into public office space; with the 'building of socialism' goes all too often the moving of filing cabinets into emptying villas and apartments.

Told it had far more space than it needed, the Lee household was all but evicted from the ground floor; this was commandeered in no time at all by the local police and the tax bureau. On the day before the night in question, a young man suspected of Kuomintang sympathies (a *very* young man, we were told by the servants, as always our eyes and ears) was brought into one of the rooms downstairs for questioning. For a good many hours the police officers gave him the third degree. He took what was coming to him; but in a brief interval in which he found himself alone, and perhaps before he had steeled himself for the next round of grilling, he thought to end it all by doing himself in.

How had he come by the pistol? No two accounts agreed. Perhaps it belonged to one of his tormentors: to instil fear during interrogations, the police agents would sometimes make a great show of unbuckling their holsters, taking out their pistols and laying them on the table – and it might have been one of those, inadvertently left in the room.

When my memory of those times is jogged, what also comes to me is a picture of my mother, head lowered over a revolver, thumb and forefinger gripping a nail file. She is in a darkened room, walled away from prying eyes by drawn curtains. She is filing, filing away the number embossed on the revolver. Her concentration on her task seems the more complete for the ambience of secrecy, of fear. Nor are her apprehensions groundless, for nobody is supposed to possess firearms any more; it is one of those things to which you have to own up, like 'ill-gotten' gains or Kuomintang connections. This has been announced, during one of those confession drives where you were promised forgiveness if you came clean. I don't know why she never turned the weapon in. Perhaps she wasn't convinced that the promise would be kept; or perhaps, slow to act, she had let the deadline pass and now it was too late. But here she is, with the deadly thing still in her possession – deadly twice over, since at any hour there can be a knock on the door, a house search by the police, and an accusation of conspiratorial designs on the state, the weapon flourished as proof.

What she must do, before she gets rid of it, is to expunge all and any marks that may allow it to be traced to her husband, who had taken out a licence for it, and whose name would therefore be on some register, inherited by the people's government. You simply can't be too careful.

I don't think my picture of her is a gloss on memory, I did come upon that scene of my mother with the revolver; but about what she did afterwards, I am only told many years later. I think it is some time during the night, her work finished to her satisfaction, that her sister's husband Eddie comes for her in his car. They drive through deserted streets, headed north for the Soochow Creek. I cannot be certain which section of the Soochow Creek they made for, though I doubt if it was any of the stretches spanned by the busy bridges to the east. I imagine them crossing a part of the city with which neither was entirely familiar. Housing thins as they leave the French Concession behind them. And then he and she are alone on a bank, and he is taking the gun from her and flinging it as far as he can into the river: wrapped in cloth and heavy, weighted down with rock.

From the days and the weeks that followed, no particular moment stands out clear in my recollection, only an atmosphere of terror and rumour – whispers of neighbours being ferreted out and taken into custody, of others being denounced or ducking down. One sensed the thinness of walls, the brittleness of windows, so that even in the dark of one's own room one no longer felt protected and unexposed. I was too young to understand what was going on, but reverberations from the adult world affected me all the same. Long after, from studying books and talking to older people, I find out that there is a likeness between all mass campaigns, and that on this occasion too, brother accused brother; son, father; those who had nursed grudges got even for each one; anonymous letters were admitted into evidence. The stakes are high; you can't be too squeamish, either you denounce or you are denounced – that is the mass campaign for you all over.

The one of which I speak was actually a case of two campaigns being rolled into one, the first succeeded so closely by the second that we all referred to them in the same breath: *sanfan, wufan*, Three-Antis, Five-Antis. I remember mouthing the slogans without the dimmest idea of what the three or the five 'poisons' were. Knowledge of what the numbers stood for was far from universal, but really it made no odds that this was so, because although they represented things like corruption and tax evasion, the categories were elastic, and you only had to have been in private business to be found guilty of one or more of them.

My uncle Eddie was later to say that he was lucky not to have come off worse than he did – at least he was not driven to the point of suicide (his younger brother was, hounded for listening to the *Voice of America*), or turfed out of his home, or sent out into the streets with a placard hanging from his neck and made to recite his sins at every corner. But that was because time had misted his memory; and because, his wife Ming said, he was temporarily unhinged by the experience and everything came to him at one remove; *she* could tell a harsher story. They are both dead now, and it is thanks to the maid Ah Sam, the one who saw to my mother's memorial service in Hong Kong, that I am able to reconstruct what happened.

Ah Sam cannot think of that time without indignation on behalf of her master and mistress – whom, had she been what she is assuredly not, a time-server, she might have washed her hands of as a losing venture. After all, is she not, as a member of the labouring class, the salt of the earth? *Her* interests are the ones the Party champions. This she understood perfectly, but it was simply not in her to cash in on it.

Ah Sam is Cantonese, as was Eddie; but while the city failed to assimilate her, so that she remained utterly herself, speaking few words of the local tongue, he was Shanghainese in all but name. Still, there was an affinity there, and she was quite devoted to him.

He was in the pharmaceutical business, an agent for American and German companies like Squibb, Merck and Schering. He was prosperous, and his house on Route H. Cordier, in the French Concession, had the feel of an extremely comfortable, well-appointed villa in the European manner: two-storeyed, parquet-floored, with a tiled patio at the back and a large apron of garden.

One evening, instead of coming home from the office by himself, he is escorted by two strangers and a number of his staff at the Nanyang Drug Company. Ah Sam counts them as they stalk in: four men, one a relative of Eddie's, a fellow-Cantonese they have had to tea; and one woman, the young Miss Li. Ah Sam registers their age, between twenty-five and thirty-five, no more; and then their roughness of manner and their crudely belligerent air. She does this without any alarm – it will take more than bullying to put *her* in a flutter.

Until just before they left the office, Eddie had no idea that they were communist. Now he is utterly at their mercy, for all over Shanghai, as part of a faultlessly conceived plan, their kind have been co-opted by the Party to grind down and finally eradicate private business. The Party let them loose on their employers, good and bad alike, whom by a remorseless process of interrogation and intimidation it is their patriotic job to Expose and Criticize. Probity ensures nothing: Eddie is a private businessman and must have something to hide – one fact presupposes the next. It is on the cards that he should be wrung like a wet cloth, wrung until all his life's earnings have seeped out. To wipe out private capital and replace it with centralized allocation is not merely to bring about socialism; it is not merely a matter of Marxist principle; it is, at its most practical, to squeeze all the money out of the rich for the national treasury to sop up.

The cook has been getting supper ready, but neither Eddie nor his wife are allowed to eat it. Indeed he is allowed nothing – no food, no cigarettes, no water, no sleep and, at first, not even to go to the lavatory. He is made to perch on a high, hard, tea table, so that he feels all his blood silting to his ankles and feet – which, after a while, he ceases to be physically aware of except as leaden appendages to which have been attached increasingly heavy weights.

'So swollen they were,' Ah Sam says of his feet many years later. 'Like *zhuti*.'

'Like what?'

'Pigs' trotters,' she repeats. She sighs, 'It was pitiful. He couldn't even walk. To so much as get up was to sway and fall. Without my helping to prop him up, he couldn't have taken a single step; couldn't even have made it to the lavatory.' Pitiable it was, a healthy six-foot-tall man like him collapsed in a heap.

From the first he and his wife are separated, to make it easier to catch them out in a lie; she is confined to her bedroom upstairs, guarded by the terrifyingly earnest Miss Li; and traffic between the two floors is strictly forbidden. Only Ah Sam comes and goes between room and room.

'Hey, you, *Guangdong ren*,' the uninvited guests shout at her. 'Get out of the way!' They call her *Guangdong ren*, 'Cantonese', in their own Shanghai dialect. She looks at them with incomprehension, affecting not to understand a word of Shanghainese, and persists in hanging about so that she can give her master a sip of the water she has sneaked in.

'What are you up to, *Guangdong ren?*' one of them exclaims on another occasion, waking up from his siesta. She is holding a cigarette to Eddie's parched lips and giving him a puff.

'Look,' she reasons with them; 'he's no good to you if he dies, is he? He's no good to you if he doesn't finish writing his confession and telling you all you want to know.'

This has to be interpreted for them by the one Cantonese speaker among the five, Eddie's relative.

All the same, they would far sooner she was out of the way: 'Get out, *Guangdong ren*! Get out of here!'

To Eddie they have been yelling, day in, night out, '*Tanbai! Tanbai!*' – Confess! Confess! – the two syllables ringing round the house.

Thus it was that *tanbai* became one of the first words to be uttered by Eddie's son, my cousin Richard, one and a half years old at the time and just beginning to speak. Another was *Haiyou? Haiyou!* – What else? Still more!

Gathered together, the sheets of paper Eddie and his wife have covered with figures and writing make up a thick wad. The most cursory reading reveals that she has the better command of political vocabulary, and from the biographical data offered it can be gleaned that she has a degree in history from a highly regarded university run on American lines. Her mind may prove, for that reason, the harder to break down. He went to Fudan – which, until its transmutation into Shanghai's topmost by the new régime, was not a university to attract the best and the brightest.

Personal particulars, company history, names and addresses of principals, bank accounts, negotiable securities – nothing has been left out. You hide nothing, because you cannot be certain if your friends or acquaintances may not have blabbed. And yet the two strangers continue to insist, 'You are withholding information. We must tell you in your own interest to make a clean breast of your past wrongdoings.' Unlike the three from the office, whom Eddie supposes to be stool-pigeons, these two are skilled interrogators, among whose gambits is the forensic one of returning again and again to the same questions, and whose look of pained impatience is designed to suggest to the interrogatee that it is high time he told them the truth, they are not the mugs he takes them for. In their ability to pounce on one's words and twist them, they are almost like barristers in a Western court of law.

Of Ah Sam they enquire, 'Have your employers maltreated you? Have they scolded you? You must tell us if they have been unkind, because this is your chance to get your own back. These are the bourgeois exploiters who have maintained the working classes in the gutter.'

The bait is not swallowed by Ah Sam, whose answer is, 'I don't know what you're talking about. If you mean by maltreatment what you're doing to the master, then no, never; such cruelty is quite unknown in this house.' She can't help adding, 'Until now.'

Eddie has come, after four days and five nights of questioning, to the state of exhaustion where he hardly knows what he is writing or saying. It is all such a long time ago. He can't understand how it has come to pass that he finds himself admitting to crimes – tax dodges, paying employees less than their due, and so on – which in his more lucid moments he would know for certain that he never committed. He is not alone in this willingness to acquiesce in the possibility of a culpability not truly his; indeed, in everything that has befallen him he is merely part of a design established across all Shanghai.

And it is in keeping with this design, too, that the departure of his interrogators should be followed by the presentation of a bill for so many years of back taxes and fines, assessed on scales so fantastically inflated that there could be no earthly hope of him ever paying it without making over all the assets of his company to the state; dismissing the chauffeur, cook and wash amah; selling the car, the fridge, his wife's jewellery, every possession of worth. He is through; bone-dry.

Will his tormentors leave it at that? No, as it not unexpectedly turns out. *His* case may be closed for the moment but here they are again, at the door, on the phone, demanding his presence at, indeed his active participation in, the denunciation of others, men in the same line of business, of whose affairs he may have inside information of use to the state. Here is his chance – what better? – to make amends for his past wrongdoings; to join in the *da laohu*, the 'tiger-bashing', would be to show himself sufficiently contrite.

No good pleading illness: they will not let him off with that. In fact he is genuinely unwell, and one cannot be certain that he may not go out of his mind if subjected to further stress. And what could be worse for one's sanity than the hysteria and violence of an Expose and Criticize meeting?

In the end it is his wife who goes, who *has* to go, with the voice on the phone barking, 'Come this instant if you know what's good for you.' She will never forget that solitary walk down the staircase, her legs wobbly, to face what there is to face – which is something still more terrible, much more terrible, in some ways, than to be denounced oneself.

You don't know from moment to moment when the call will come – at dawn, past midnight, or just as you are sitting down to your supper. Ah Sam remembers: 'She'd be gone all day.' Coming home wan and wilfully silent. From her outward calmness it cannot be guessed what she has been through. Nor where she has

gone – mass meetings have been called all over town: at the old
Cercle Sportif Français, the Race Course, in any space where
thousands may gather. She says to no one then (but to me many
years later) that the experience utterly undid her fear, bred all
helplessness out of her. From then on she would always have
what it takes, the power to suffer without shrivelling.

At home, impoverishment, plus by and by the rationing
system, means congee on the dinner table in place of steamed
rice. To make the congee palatable – since there is nothing
whatever to go with it, not an egg, not a pickle – Ah Sam learns
to lace it with a spoonful of glucose from the bottles left over
from the Nanyang Drug Company. In the closets, the few outfits
that remain will now see service year after year.

I giggle to see people foreshortened into dwarfs as they stand in
front of the convex mirrors in the aisles of the Great World. I am
having the time of my life, bumping my way up this amusement
palace, floor by floor, with my sister and brother ahead and
beside me, Nanny Moon and Hanze somewhere behind, and
shoals of people trailing children all around. Throngs fill such
space as is not taken up by shooting galleries, peep shows, mazes,
gaming tables, slot machines, tea rooms, photographers' booths,
opera performances, orchestras, lottery sellers, story tellers,
pingtan balladeers, trapeze artists and acrobats. This last group
particularly entrances me; and I am spellbound by the way one
little girl, her legs on her shoulders, keeps saucers twirling, faster
and faster, on sticks balanced on her head and feet.

It is dark when we come out of the Great World and saunter
down Avenue Eduoard VII. Here the wicked old Shanghai seems
not to have receded an inch; the revolution might never have
been. Here the Sin City lives again, among the women, some
young, some more than a shade past their prime, sidling up to the

male passers-by on the pavements. I am not aware of them at first, though if pointed out to me I could, even then, have supplied their name with ease. They are called *yeji*, wild chickens – which will suggest the nature of their calling. (I knew about streetwalkers from a very early age; it came of living in Shanghai, reputed to have more prostitutes than any city in the world, and of being so much around servants, which made for a curious combination of ignorance and precocity.)

As we amble down Avenue Edouard VII, my only awareness is of a drama suddenly being enacted around me, an affair of minutes only – raised voices, scuffling, staring faces, someone making a spurt, a figure giving chase, women being herded past a long line of murmuring onlookers into a waiting van, an excitement breathing over the street. All these impressions float to the surface of my memory like scraps of wreckage, not focused or made sense of until the reminiscences of others and the records of newspapers have supplied the context which the original experience lacked.

I now know that what I witnessed was the rounding-up of the city's prostitutes by the plain-clothes police, part of a mopping-up exercise which went on, with pauses, for a good eight years. The first swoop (at 8 p.m. on 25 November 1951) had emptied neither the singsong houses nor the red-light districts – how could it, Shanghai was saturated with the trade? – and a second and third were made in succeeding years. Police agents in disguise pounced in hotels, massage parlours, amusement arcades, on skating rinks, from the shadows of a hundred streets and alleys. Brothel keepers and pimps faced the firing squad. In eight years, I read, a little over 7,500 women were trawled – a number large enough, but not so as to suggest a root-and-branch extirpation; even in the New China, one cannot see this business closing for good and all. Flesh for hire did not, as the propaganda would have it, become entirely a thing of the past; but the world of the singsong house was no more.

So far as all that was concerned, Shanghai was as dead as the moon; snuffed out were not just loucheness and debauchery, but also variety, colour, glitter, gaiety, temptation, the desires evoked in one by sensuous display. Multifariousness was no more, so that instead of each person having a Shanghai of his own, made up of sub-worlds of this and that, there was now one Shanghai for everyone, monolithic. One fell in with the new puritanism, and did so with increasing fatalism and diminishing regret. When I look back I see myself in a blue boiler suit, cut one size too big to allow margin for growth (I thought it the fashion then, since people called it *gongren zhuang*, 'workers' suit', and workers were the bee's knees). I see sartorial greyness, collars and lapels without so much as a bas-relief Lenin brass badge to adorn them. I see necklaces unclasped, brooches unpinned, flowers unworn, faces unmade-up, the ballrooms closed, the waltzes and foxtrots undanced, the neon unlit . . . And, against these, an image from an older day, never to be conjured up in Shanghai again: a woman caped in chinchilla, one white-gloved hand resting on a mahogany rail.

The familiar city receded from us, shifting further away every day. In time we ceased to keep a look-out for the street vendors we recognized by particular cries or ditties and, no less, smells. Everything was on its way out. The itinerant cooks with their wheeled kitchens. The sweet makers who blew boiled syrup into whatever shape was asked for – pig or bird, car or boat, leaf or gourd, fan or comb. All vanished. Ice-cold prune juice. Piping hot sweet potatoes. Cool fermented white rice. Eggs stewed in brown tea. Golden doughnut twists. Roasted chestnuts. Candied red apples. Dates stuffed with nougat. Rank fermented beancurd. Noodles in soup. Mince-filled dumplings both steamed and pan-fried. The walnut-porridge seller held out the longest, then disappeared with all the rest, his ditty swallowed up by silence on Route Winling:

> *Duk! Duk! Duk!*
> *Sugared purée for sale.*
> *Three catties of walnut,*
> *Four catties of shell.*
> *You have the nut,*
> *I'll have the shell.*

11

My father had a gift for friendship and made friends easily. Apart from Max Minutti, he was close to Jesse. He liked to do things with Jesse, dances, races, tennis parties, riding, flirting with older women, annoying people by laughing loudly and making wild and witty talk in restaurants and teahouses, the kind of thing you could do with dash because you were young enough, carefree enough, and because you needed to do it.

Jesse had an equable disposition and went along with nearly everything my father suggested, including the proposition that they lose their virginity. By the prevailing standards of what was fitting they were too young for it, but once decided upon, my father went at the project with a lively explorer's relish. At tea dances and in ballrooms he enjoyed all the success that a boy in his teens could have wished for. And so the lines of his life were set. It was a measure of his flair, of how much he charmed, that among themselves some of Shanghai's most sought-after dance hostesses vied to be the first to 'taste the broiler', as I believe the expression went, the first to have the lad for a lover. 'Come after hours,' Li Mana whispered in his ear, she whom men queued up to dance with at the Majestic Nightclub. 'That way you won't have to pay.' His standards were not high but would grow higher.

With Jesse it was quite different: no sooner was he faced with his first woman than he went cold and limp; and that shrivelling sensation was to stay with him. The books that Father sent Hanze off to Fuzhou Road to buy were no help, not even the ones with the explicit pictures, while Jesse's mildness of manner precluded any resort to initiative or boldness on the part of the women. At first my father attempted consolation, then judged that what Jesse needed was a doctor, the very best that Shanghai could offer. It was typical of him that, lacking the money to pay for his friend's treatment – Jesse didn't have a penny – he should ask his father for it, risking the old man's wrath. He had to own up, explain what the two of them had been up to, but if he had to put himself out for friendship's sake, he would. For his part my grandfather kept his misgivings to himself, expressing a distant well-wishing and giving more than was needed; that boy of his was spoiled all right, but at least he was not a milksop.

'Poor Jesse,' my father said to me more than forty years after the event (in 1984). 'You see, he was a posthumous child; he grew up without a father figure; his mother cossetted him, since he was all she had.'

When he told me this we were driving from Vancouver to the Okanagan Valley, some seven or eight hours to the southeast. I'd been summoned from London to keep him company in a log cabin he'd had built there (for his retirement, he said) and had complied out of a vague sense of filial duty.

My father had just been in San Francisco to see his Shanghainese friends, the ones who'd got out of China in 1949, but instead of going on to the casinos in Las Vegas he had plumped for a secluded holiday in the cabin. Besides our luggage, the car carried eight roast ducks from a Cantonese restaurant in Vancouver to see us through our fortnight in the wilds. Not that, as a Shanghainese, my father liked Cantonese food, his taste buds were that parochial; but it was all he could get in Vancouver, and it was still preferable to anything European or American.

The reason my father brought up Jesse was that, through a chance remark by somebody at a dinner party he'd gone to in San Francisco, he had learned that his friend was alive and well and living in Seattle. There was no mistaking his excitement at this discovery; he was tempted to change his travel plans and fly at once to Seattle. When we pulled up at a roadside eatery he all but bounded up the drive, nearly slipping on the crust of frozen snow.

The furnishings of the room we entered had been chosen for their qualities of endurance, and a dreary dun colour predominated. I found it deeply depressing, but my father was abstracted, faraway. Indeed he hardly noticed what he ate, helping himself to unpromising English chips from a proffered bowl. 'I can't wait to get in touch with Jesse.' Then, noticing a phone on a far wall, he said, 'Now's as good a time as any,' and asked me for all my quarters. He must have been in luck with directory enquiries because he was all smiles when he returned to our table. He had dialled the Seattle number and Jesse himself had answered the phone, Jesse of whom he had had no news for close on forty years.

'Well,' I said, 'did he ever overcome his difficulty?'

My father considered a moment before answering. 'It seems Jesse was married for a while. An American woman. But it didn't last, I don't know why.' There was a short pause before he said, 'There were no children.'

Then he flashed me a smile and said he and Jesse would meet on his next trip to America. He spoke excitedly of his plans for their reunion.

Much later, looking back, I remember my own tingle of pleasure at the thought of the two friends meeting, after so many years apart. But in the event the reunion never happened; for a few weeks after he and I took leave of each other, he to fly home via the Pacific, I to cross the Atlantic for London, my father died of a stroke in Malaysia. Time was not on his side.

My mother had less need of friends or of general human company; she was less ready to find amusement in a foible, and was one of those people who could live contentedly within themselves. (Sitting up in bed, accepting the near approach of death, she occupied herself for hours doing crosswords.) Such self-sufficiency is sometimes forced on people who feel them-selves different from those by whom they are surrounded. On how many evenings, in Malaysia and Hong Kong, had I watched her making conversation with women – wives of my father's friends or business associates – whose mental life was entirely enclosed, as hers was assuredly not, by everyday practical concerns?

Of some women I heard her say, 'The trouble with people who have nothing to do is that they waste other people's time.' She was never malicious, but she could tear people to ribbons. At times my father had cause to think her a snob. He also knew that she had the capacity to deal with matters that he himself could merely regret or bewail. He knew she was the stronger. I don't think I ever saw her sitting with her hands clasped and her head bowed – she had never been glimpsed in an attitude of defeat. She was one of those people who could go through life step by step, for whom what happens happens, and that is that. She never regretted the wrong things. She was the sort who, when she looked back on her life, could scarcely think of anything she wished undone.

I have often wondered what she thought of her husband – that is, as distinct from what she loved in him. Her love for my father was on a different scale from that of the rest of the loves in her life. Her love for him, in comparison to which all other loves seemed small, made orphans of her children. He was the maypole, the pivot around which we were all made to revolve. She made it impossible for us, as children, to refer to him as being in any degree fallible. From her feelings for my father I learned that you can forgive a person any number of faults for one endearing quality, for a certain style – while someone with many virtues may become insupportable for a single imperfection if it happens to be a boring one.

After she died and people assessed the hand that Fate had dealt her – the way the Chinese like to do with those freshly dead – almost everyone judged her lot to have been a happy one. Her husband was good to her, they said; he might have amused himself casually with other women but she always came first with him. He saw their marriage as an unbreakable bond; she was one person he would never leave. On every anniversary of her death he would fly to London to be at her grave – 'To render my annual report,' he would say. It was a gesture of devotion as of respect. Above all, he begrudged her nothing – a Chinese man is rated a good husband if he doesn't stint his wife of housekeeping money. He was generous to himself and to others, incapable of penny-pinching.

It wasn't then, but later, that I wondered how much it really weighed with her, the fact that she wanted for nothing materially. It wasn't then, but later, that I properly grieved for her.

We may be convulsed by lesser pangs, but grief of the highest charge comes to us wrapped in a muffling coat of unreality; we may tremble at the first shock, but that trembling must continue through the years before the charge is dissipated. This was not clear to me all at once; realization came on that first trip back to

China, which rejoined me to the flow of past experience and struck some spring of hidden sadness.

It began with my visit to the house in Shanghai where my mother had grown up. In Carter Road, as it used to be called, I tracked down her mother. Grandma Lee was living in what used to be the storeroom, a dark and icy attic above the servants' quarters. Years ago she was told by those who came to take possession of the family house that one must swim with the times, especially if one was a former capitalist. But the times would cease to involve her interest as, with the passing years, the world around her seemed to grow more and more demented. One day a Red Guard raised his hand to her and, even as she drew back in fear, struck her hard across the face. In such a world, the quiet daily routine became the only way she knew of living. She took this sort of life as it came and did not think too much about it or about anything.

As I stood at the top of the flight of steps leading to the attic, I found her gazing out at me through an open door. She was sitting at a high square table, her hands making clasping movements, chapped with cold. She was all in black and looked as fragile as dried leaves. Her spine had frozen into a perfect arc, so that it was in the posture of a shrimp that she shuffled from one end of the room to the other, picking things up and dropping them. She was eighty-three but in full possession of all her faculties. Her ears and eyes were still sharp.

'That mother of yours,' she said of her youngest daughter; 'it's years since that mother of yours wrote to me.'

'She is unfilial,' I said, my heart stricken. I couldn't bring myself to utter aloud the words that rang in my ears: *She is dead, she is dead*.

'Is your father good to her?' She meant by 'good' something like materially solicitous. The question whether happiness was in any way connected with love would not have suggested itself to one of her generation.

'Yes,' I said truthfully with one side of me: he was too, an exemplary husband by every test save one. But with another side of me I saw him as failing her, denying her his fidelity.

'She asked me to give you this,' I lied, proffering a wad of *yuan*. The fingers of Grandma Lee's right hand emerged from the long sleeve of her padded tunic to take it from me. I noticed that they were stippled with liver spots. After they had laid the money aside they retreated back into the sleeve – one way of warming oneself in a room that, in a winter every bit as cold as England's, had no heating whatsoever.

I couldn't help asking, 'Are you warm enough?' – stiff and wretched with cold myself. I looked about me and mentally put on a fire in that terrible room. It is a north-facing room, sunless whatever the time of day. It exuded a sense of dereliction, made worse by the fillets of feeble light seeping through the windows.

Save her, I prayed, save her from being bruised. I wanted to comfort her, or myself, but her gaze, mild and unblinking, sought no consolation, and in any case I could not find the words. It occurred to me that I might be a token drifting in from a world she had done with, a token to which she could not be troubled to attach any meaning. There were no grounds for believing that my return would count more than a little with her. She had long supposed, with good reason, that she would never see me again, and her existence had assumed a form to which I was superfluous.

That night my sleep was shallow and disturbed, broken by dreams. Strangely, I dreamed not of the grandmother I had just seen, but of the one I never knew – she who occupies a place in my mind larger and more deeply graven than that of many people I know. She is tilting a cup. She might have been washing something down, or trying to drown her sorrows. I am gripping her by her shoulders, and when she wheels round, cup emptied, I cannot get over the impression that it is my mother I am grasping. The face is unfamiliar, and yet I seem to have known it. The two women are blurred together, my mother and my father's mother. The past has lost all chronology, coming and going in jumbled fragments.

I awoke in the small hours, feverish and ill. I felt a severe pain in my throat and chest, and when I raised myself on my elbows an attack of coughing came upon me with such violence that I was left exhausted and dazed. I had been suffering fits of coughing for some days – I'd put it down to a cold and the sooty air of Shanghai – but none of these attacks had come in such juddering force as this.

I got up and staggered to the bathroom, feeling cold and emptied. The spasms returned, and as I leaned shuddering over the washbasin, supporting myself with my palms on the rim, I observed that I was bringing up gobbets of blood. Panic now rose to my throat, and I thought with alarm, I am quite sick, I'll never get away from this dreadful place, never.

I fell limp into bed and stretched rigid across it, like a plank, for a few moments. I was conscious of my thoughts, disconnected at first, shaping themselves in a way I did not wish. I shifted to my side and, as if to bury the unwelcome thoughts, pressed my face into the pillow and slid up my arm to encircle my head. Then all at once I started to weep without restraint, and was surprised to hear my voice cry, 'Mother' aloud.

The thought that came unbidden was large and simple: *she had wanted to die*. She had felt more cheated than anyone suspected – she was good at concealing how much she minded. This I had known from the very beginning, but I had refused the knowledge. Not knowing had made it all endurable. Now I felt myself to be without resource against the inadmissible, as grief overswept me in the fullness of its power.

I waited for the night to pass. I thought it impossible that I would sleep, but a little while before daybreak I fell precipitously into oblivion as into a bottomless pit, and slept on and on until suddenly it was midday and the telephone was ringing.

It was Hanze. I told him I had a fever. I thought, probably – certainly – he would come to the hotel at once.

In no time at all he was beside me, calling my name. I opened my eyes and in my weakness and self-pity was tearfully grateful to see his face drawn in solicitude and anxiety. There was a woman with him, who seemed by her manner to be a nurse. I heard them murmur, their heads together, 'Bronchitis.'

At the Huadong Hospital, where I next found myself, I heard Hanze speak in my ear, 'Built by your grandfather.' I smiled to think that, had we been sightseeing, he'd have given me exact figures, costs, profits or losses. I looked up at a high window too grimy to see through. It must be Shanghai's best hospital, I thought, it's where they send foreign visitors. That's what I am by virtue of my British passport, a foreigner. The same passport required that I be accompanied on this occasion by a minder from the China International Travel Service, one whose job it was simply to hang about. This man gave me a look of apology each time a bout of coughing convulsed me.

I remember only very indistinctly that I was given an injection. Then, wishing to be alone, I asked to be taken back. I already felt better, knowing I was past those waves of panic that sick people are prey to.

A drizzle blurred the windshield of the taxi which returned me to the hotel. In the car Hanze said: 'You shouldn't be at the hotel all by yourself; you should come home with me and let me and my old woman look after you, wait on your needs.' I smiled weakly at him, shaking my head. If Hanze had anything to do with it, I'd be taken to their one-roomed flat, occupy their only bed, the one Hanze shared with his wife and daughter, and be ministered to by the three of them, day and night if need be. They would put their own concerns aside, their pleasures sacrificed, their own discomforts and tiredness discounted while they applied themselves wholeheartedly to nursing me. For Hanze it went without saying that they should all go sleepless so that I, who had a bed to go to, might have someone to turn to at any hour.

I told him, 'No, I shall be perfectly all right in the hotel.' Besides, my panic had given way to a childish relief, a sense that the matter had somehow been taken out of my hands.

'You need to have someone with you,' he said with gentle persistence when we arrived at the door. Nothing could have affected me so poignantly as the humility with which he added, hesitantly, 'You would greatly oblige me by allowing me to watch over you.' It did not seem possible to refuse him.

That night I slept and woke and slept again. I was vaguely conscious of the room growing dark and then growing light. I was aware of Hanze's extraordinarily silent presence, as reassuring, and as oddly familiar, as a dog that nightly takes its post at one's feet. If I woke from one of my dozes during the night I always saw him sitting in a chair in the darkness, his hands folded and his eyes open.

12

I am stone deaf in one ear and, lying in bed on my good side, did not hear the phone ring. My house-guest Evelyn took the call from my sister-in-law and came into my bedroom to break the news to me. My father had suffered a stroke. Dead and gone, at one stroke.

I had imagined, in advance, the ways in which that news might reach me – in a solemn or matter-of-fact voice, from the mouth of a physician or a relative, at home or in a strange country. But experience of this kind can seldom be forestalled. Reality is always more than one bargains for.

I understood that the seizure and death had occurred in the span of an hour, and I reflected: Good, that'll have been quick enough for him; he would have hated to have lived to wither and disintegrate, to have been dead alive.

I made ready to leave London for Singapore at once, for although my father had died in Malaysia, it was in Singapore that he was to be cremated – it was easier for everyone to congregate in Singapore, the place with the international airport.

It'll be steamy there, I thought, and I have nothing to wear that's both cool and black; and then was incredulous that such normal observations could cross my mind at a moment like this. I talked about this to Evelyn, who is a barrister and had plenty of black clothes to lend me. 'Here, have this,' she said, and I packed a black cotton blouse of hers. On my way to Heathrow Airport, I foresaw, absurdly, the sense of oppression that having to carry my heavy winter coat would cause me once I arrived in the sweltering heat of Singapore.

I landed at Changi International Airport a little ahead of the coffin. My brother had accompanied the body and I saw him appear in the arrivals hall when it was being unloaded from the aeroplane. He crossed the room when he spotted me and put one arm around my shoulders, wordlessly. His other hand clutched a briefcase containing documentation for clearing the coffin through customs. An airline officer came to take the papers from him, and I wondered, again absurdly, how they listed corpses on the manifest. How we'd get through the next days, on the other hand, I could not begin to think.

Niangniang had been the first to arrive, flown in by Qantas from Sydney. She was pacing up and down the hall and dabbing at her eyes, wailing, 'Who'd have thought he'd go before I, who'd have thought it?' I looked at her and I thought, You'll outlive us all. I could see that we'd have to make a point of not encouraging Niangniang in her public display of emotion. If we were not careful we'd have her lamenting all night: she knew the words, she'd known them since childhood.

Didi, the name by which my brother is known to all the family, gave the name of our hotel when we got into a taxi. I don't now recall what it was, because it made no odds with me where we were to be put up, Hilton or Shangri-La or Sheraton: those international-style hotels all seemed the same to me.

I understood that the coffin would be taken from the airport straight to the funeral parlour – where, somewhat late in the day, the body was to be embalmed.

The Singapore Casket Company, standing amidst car-repair shops on Lavender Street, had four parlours, in one of which the body of my father awaited its rites. When we went there the next morning, we found no reception desk, only a notice board with Father's name, and two others, pinned up by the lift. One parlour I passed was provided with tables and tablecloths, so that those who kept vigil might play cards or mah-jong if they wished. 'Chinese will be Chinese,' I observed. There were rails on the walls from which to hang condolence blankets, a gift traditionally given at funerals to betoken the bringing of warmth to the coldly dead.

Something in me shrank from the viewing of the body, though I had wanted to look on my father one last time. A panel of the lid of the coffin had been lifted to reveal the face, framed by ruched silk. The face was in good shape, but it was wider, flatter, not the one I knew. But for the hair, it could have been a mask carved from wax.

You can never be embalmed, I reflected, to the likeness of life, thinking that this was also true of the only other embalmed body I'd seen, that of Mao Zedong in the mausoleum in Peking.

Deliberately summoning memories, I had a picture of the sitting room in the log cabin in British Columbia where my father and I spent our last holiday together, of the shining white light of the snow as I saw it through the windows, of the blazing logs in the fireplace, and of the expression on my father's face, with the mouth set and the gaze faraway, which he always wore when he was watching television. They were long, those winter evenings. They had about them a feel of great repose and completeness. The cabin itself seemed so restful it was almost possible to think of it as a home and not as a place of exile.

Most of the time we had no other company. This would not normally have suited my father, but he was not gregarious that winter. Odd, that he should have seemed so content with the quiet pattern of our days, the drives into the mountains, the walks around the frozen lakes, the evenings by the fire, the lulling sense of routine. Is he getting old, I found myself wondering, solitude had never appealed to him before? It was the only trip he ever made to North America, I think, which didn't include a stop in Las Vegas. We never talked much but that solitude, and that immaculate snow, and that perfect silence all around locked us in a sympathy new and I think precious to us both. In my recollections those days have assumed a simple perfection, and but for their memory his death would have left me feeling unendurably bereft.

Seeing us together that winter, you might have taken us for friends. We felt, I think, something like the rough intimacy of travellers. With him I was less compliant than others dared to be, and I think he liked me for standing up to him. In all the years I had known him it was the only time I ever felt a power over him, a power that came of knowing that he needed my approval, perhaps even more than I needed his.

All this, now, I summoned up, standing by the casket. I knew I had to wait, perhaps for a long time, for my father's death to become real to me. I dwelt, for a moment, on this, then stepped back as I became aware of people speaking in low voices around me. Sleepiness thickened the haze in which I noted the arrival of callers and the delivery of wreaths. I was grateful for the orthodox condolences, which required only orthodox answers. To those charged with delivering the flowers my brother responded as was proper, dishing out *hongbao*, gifts of money in auspicious red paper packets. I didn't know the etiquette and was surprised that Didi did. Some of those who came to pay their last respects sat down to pass a few minutes in silence, in blue plastic chairs that stood in rows facing the casket, letting a decent interval elapse before they took their leave of us. As the minutes ticked by I waited for the shiftings in seats and the glances at watches.

The most restless person there was in fact Niangniang, harbouring an operatic protest in her breast. She was finding the whole thing offensively muted: she wanted noise, she wanted mourners swaying and keening over a bier, flinging themselves forward, tearing at their clothes, grasping their dishevelled hair.

When the undertakers came to screw down the lid of the coffin, Didi said that we'd do this ourselves, recalling how our father had hammered home the stoppers of *his* father's casket. It was time now for Didi to be his father's son. I dimly remember someone handing me a screwdriver. Getting the screwdriver to turn properly was a struggle for one with as little co-ordination between hand and eye as me, one to whom games, for instance, have always been a mortification. I laughed at my own clumsiness. Laughing over his dead body? He'd have laughed at me himself.

The cremation was the following morning. Didi and Niangniang said they'd sit up through the night in the funeral parlour, and I left them to return to the hotel. I was still on London time, and fell into a heavy sleep at once.

All I remember of the Mount Vernon Crematoria is the aisle-like driveways, the shaven lawns extending on each side of the approach, a Malay employee telling me, because I'd asked, that it took three hours for a body to burn.

During the ceremony we all sat facing the coffin, which looked smaller, somehow, than you would expect: a doll's box with frills inside. It struck me that if this were England they'd have asked us to choose some music to play at the point the coffin slid through the curtains, and we wouldn't have known what to pick; my father did not listen to music and was quite incapable of carrying a tune. In England I'd not have to go down on my knees with my brother and knock my head on the floor before the coffin; there wouldn't have been a Chinese audience to expect it of me. In any case I'd have felt phoney, whereas here, oddly, it was both appropriate and natural. Kowtowing to my father, I felt I was making amends for my inadequacies as a daughter.

The ceremony was brief and plain and I reflected that my father, who liked things ritzy, would have deplored it as meagre and unseemly. But Didi had said that he would come to London with the ashes next year for burial next to our mother's and we would make an occasion of it then – something fitting, done as handsomely as our father would have wished. My father had seen to it that the headstone he raised for his wife, seven years before, was engraved with his own epitaph as well; all that would remain for his children to do would be to add the date of death and to have the red characters painted black. Everything was prepared.

Niangniang let it be known that she was displeased. 'Where's the *xibo*?' she hissed. She meant the piles of tinfoil paper, folded in the shape of the silver nuggets used as money in imperial China, that one burned at funerals. My father was not being given a decent send-off, unaccompanied by a prodigality of smoking joss money.

My brother saved the day by saying, quite gravely, 'It's all right, Niangniang, we're burning all his credit cards, his American Express, Visa, MasterCard and so on; and we're burning his favourite possession of all, what he could most do with in the other life.'

A stay-at-home would want his books or slippers. An addict of air travel, such as my father was, would want his carry-on luggage. Didi had thought to bring his Pierre Cardin overnight bag from Malaysia. Of the softest leather, compact yet capacious, this had gone everywhere with him, and now would be safely airborne in flames.

Out in the drive, where hands were shaken and departure prolonged out of politeness, I looked to see who was there. I recognized my father's two closest friends – Mr Chang, one of a very few people from Shanghai to live in Singapore; and Mr Fan, who had flown in from Hong Kong for the funeral. Their wives were standing about, not facing one another but none the less making a pair, as the two best-groomed women there. Mrs Chang was the more heavily made-up of the two, but Mrs Fan was the one with the salon highlights in her wavy hair. I was touched that Mrs Fan had to gulp down a sob during the service.

On the other side of the drive, Didi and Mr Fan were conferring, two tall men with heads lowered to one another. They seemed to be speaking in undertones, as though exchanging confidences. I did not foresee that the disclosure of these that evening would thump me in the gut like the downward lurch of an aeroplane.

I heard somebody say of the deceased, 'He completed his Chinese cycle of sixty, the cycle of Cathay: is this not indeed a fate worthy of envy?' Niangniang said, 'He had earned it, the dispatch with which his life was ended.' She meant, he had done no evil for which he had had to pay by a long drawn-out death; he had accrued enough merit to remain lucid and himself to the end.

'What will you have?' I asked Niangniang in the hotel coffee shop that evening.

'Wahng,' she said.

'What?'

'Wahng,' Niangniang repeated, '*hongjiu*.'

'Oh wine,' I said, assimilating the term to the three or four other words of English which Niangniang spoke. We all knew what these words were – for some reason they were 'enjoy', 'jealous', 'lonely'.

We ate our Hainanese chicken rice and Singapore fried noodles, while Niangniang drank. She used to smoke her cigarettes through a long holder but had now given that up.

'Quite a bibber, aren't you?' I teased her.

'I know how to *enjoy* life,' Niangniang said, using another one of her English words.

'Wow,' said Didi, affecting awe at the size of her English vocabulary. Just then we were glad to have Niangniang with us; she was the distraction we needed, our buffer against tears.

She was no stranger to the pleasure of good living, 'Not like you lot,' she said in a supercilious tone. 'You people begrudge yourselves. Not me.' Abstemiousness is not prized, material indulgence is. She has a hard time keeping cooks in the house. She is quite unable to trust anybody's intelligence, and very forthright in commenting on the lack of it, always in her most acerbic vocabulary.

'What does it mean to enjoy life?' I asked a little sententiously, thinking there were many things I could and did appreciate, for which people like Niangniang would never credit me.

'Eating well –' Niangniang began. 'I know what you're thinking: you're thinking, How shallow. But one day you'll discover that if you want a good time it's best to seek it in food – what else is left?' What more mattered? All else was vanity. Dust and ashes and emptiness.

I envied Niangniang her certitude but her view of life appalled me. I would have liked to tell her that she had got it wrong, that satisfaction for the belly was not the same as sustenance for the spirit. To tell her that life was not like that, that it was – what? Hers was the view of a person of an older and wearier culture than the one which, living all those years in the West, I had absorbed to perhaps a greater degree than I had suspected.

She shrugged, then changed the subject. 'I don't know about you lot but I'm going to have rites performed for your father. In China. Perhaps in Shanghai, at the Jade Buddha Temple.'

'Better things to do,' I said. If she had anything to do with it, it would not be a simple one-day affair: she'd order the works, with the full complement of monks reciting sutras for the maximum number of days.

'You go and do it if you like, Niangniang,' I said. 'Count me out.'

For some time we looked down into our bowls. I knew that our minds were not on the things we talked of. In our different ways we were all thinking of the young woman who appeared the night Didi and Niangniang sat up in the funeral parlour. It can't be said that they were completely taken by surprise, because Didi had learned of her existence from Mr Fan a few hours before (why is it that the people most concerned always hear last?) and had warned Niangniang.

Mr Fan had said only two things. 'Your father had a mistress.' And, 'They have a son; he's barely one.'

And then she was there.

Mr Fan had seen to it that she arrived in Singapore from Hong Kong in time for the viewing of the body. Niangniang, one of her brows rising a very little, glanced up when she appeared in the doorway; then instantly took her eyes off the woman. Before Didi could be sure what he thought of her she was gone.

'Dry-eyed, she was,' Niangniang later reported. 'Well, of course she never loved him,' she added. 'Gave me a turn.'

'What did?'

'All that banging. The doors swinging to at the moment of her arrival. As though your father's ghost was trying to tell me something.'

Her name was Sina, and she was younger than me. Who was she? We were curious – how not? But we did not find out then. Nor did we find out much about her in a year, in two, three or four years.

I was kept in the dark until after the funeral, by which time she'd left Singapore. On being told by Didi I felt astonishment, dismay, reproof and a disproportionate foreboding. *A child.* Amongst all I had thought of, so far as I had allowed myself to think at all, I had not thought of this.

I felt the past, and dreaded the future. A parallel came horribly pat to mind, and struck me like a thunderclap. I couldn't help it, the drag of imagination backward, to that meeting with Yeshu in Canton; and back further, to my grandfather . . . to his death and the revelation of another son's existence. All at once all that, everything, rose in my mind and hit me. It's all a chain, I thought with sickening conviction, an inescapable chain.

Niangniang hated me when I said, 'Like father, like son.'

Next day we all travelled to our home town in Malaysia. In a place that is not home I have been homesick for this place that is not home either. Passing years have changed it: mangrove had been sliced down, swamps filled in. The wilderness has retreated, and I found I could quite easily persuade myself to believe in the habitability of the place. On a ring of water left by a tumbler on a tabletop, ants no longer close in, checking for sugar.

Niangniang had said, 'Your father's clothes would go down well in China,' that Oxfam of *émigré* Chinese; and the house-keeper and I now busied ourselves sorting them out and packing them for dispatch to the Chusan Archipelago. We opened cupboards, rummaged in drawers. I smiled to think of our country cousins, with their cracked feet and torn hands, got up in suits and ties.

It did not take long, sorting out my father's personal things. There was no disorderly past to reach back into, no letters, photographs, brochures, receipts, not a scrap of paper to record his private life – there were only the files in his office, charting his business life. Whoever came looking for my father's past in this room would be shocked to find how little there was of it. Indeed the bare impersonality of his bedroom denied that he had ever existed.

'Is that it?' the housekeeper presently asked, surveying an empty closet.

'No, there's that,' I said, pointing to a drawer in one corner of the bedroom. I walked across and opened it and all at once I was shivering.

In the exact centre of an otherwise empty drawer, looking as though they harboured secrets, lay two sets of yellowing paper, folded in half and bound with thread, like booklets. Without knowing why, I was seized with a sudden dread. I took the booklets out of the drawer and went into the dining room with them, and then I sat at the table and began turning the pages.

They were two horoscopes, one written out with a brush, the other with a fountain pen. They had clearly been cast by two different men, at two different times. I scanned the prophesies, fleetingly taking in references to the important events of my father's life – marriage, birth of son (but not daughter), rise and fall of material fortunes – and the age at which each was ordained to take place. I noted the years of intermittent felicity.

My eyes hurried on to the last page. I saw that neither horoscope went beyond the sixtieth year. I read the final entries, to find out the length of time given my father to live. And it was then that I learned my father's other secret, his hidden fear. He had known he was going to die, or at least had half believed his life would end (as it indeed did) in its sixty-second year. The last nine characters of one horoscope read:

Alas, sir, when you complete your cycle of sixty,
You shall see only two more springs.

The other forecast, too, told him that death lay in wait for him; that he had no time to lose after sixty, when *the water flows and the flowers fade, speeding you on your way*. His margin of doubt, if he had any, was a matter of months, not years.

It was no good telling myself this was absurd, mere super-stition, because the point was not whether I believed in the prophecy, but whether he did. My father was a person who believed that no man can outrun his destined end; to him his death must have seemed intended, ordained – how many times had I heard him speak of the lot apportioned to men, and of his own as 'the unhappy fate allotted me'?

How is it to have one's destiny opening out before one like this, in measured periods of good fortune and bad? Did he think, It will be over quite soon now? Did he, knowing the time, wonder about the place and the manner? Did he ask, What am I to suffer? The future was not a blankness, unforeseeable and without dread. It had an ominous hold on him, a darkness into which he was already falling.

Looking again at the horoscopes, my eyes were drawn to a sentence I'd missed the first time round. It read: 'Two sons will survive you.'

But what riveted the eye, what transfixed my mind and gave the moment the character of revelation, was the question mark pencilled next to the sentence. I stared at it with a cold and startled sense of acquiring knowledge I'd sooner be without.

I imagined my father puzzling over the statement – wasn't Didi the only son he had, the other having died in infancy? The truth of the prophecy must have struck him later, with the birth of the child by Sina. Or was it a case of his falling in with the prophecy, out of some wish to test the veracity of the horoscope as a whole? Did the pattern emerge, or did he put the pattern in? How much more store must he have set by that other augury, the one of his death, when this one all but confounded reason by coming true: if this could be foretold, then so could that; if one omen held, then so might another. The birth of the child must have shaped itself into a portent of his death, a terrible presage and fulfilment.

'Gives me the creeps,' I said to my brother, who had joined me at the dining table. I showed him the horoscopes.

'If you anticipate things,' he said, hitting the nail on the head, 'they happen.' My father could well have thought, If one accepts one's fate, one must go to meet it.

Didi walked round the dining table and stared out of the window. 'He did tell me, come to think of it, that this was going to be a perilous year for him. I didn't know what he meant.' My father was never one to tell all his mind, as we were discovering – after a person dies is when you find out the most fundamental things about him, when the complexities of his life unravel.

When I was alone again I reminded myself of the matter of the child, which did not bear going into but which we had better take in hand.

He was only just in time to fulfil that prophecy, I said to myself. To Didi, though, I was never to mention that bit of the horoscope again, as though some things are best not spoken of, lest you give them power.

13

I was in for some sticky moments. In Hong Kong, where I stayed for a fortnight before returning to London, I had telephoned Sina and suggested a meeting. Meeting one's father's mistress seemed to me to call for a certain prowess; it demanded flair and I doubted that I should be equal to the challenge. I didn't know how such a meeting was to be borne and how one was not to behave like a prig.

I had got Sina's number from Mr Fan, who despite being taciturn succeeded in conveying the impression that I should be prepared to find myself a little, but no more than a little, perturbed by her. He was not explicit, but I was given to understand that one thing I needn't expect was jiggery-pokery. Nor, it seemed, was Sina the sort to cry for the moon. She appeared to have been the ideal kept woman, decorative, pliable, unexigent, a sort of licensed hanger-on who could be summoned at short notice and who would be there whenever she was needed. It was hard to get more than a few of my questions answered by Mr Fan, mostly because they were unaskable (what was she before she met Father, a dance hostess, one may take it?) and because I feared having the burden of knowing all the details; I shrank from involvement.

The bare facts were that my father had set her up in a flat and would go there most evenings, though by no means all, he found himself in Hong Kong. It wasn't exactly a hole-and-corner life for her, because they went out to restaurants and even, once or twice, travelled together; his closest friends knew her, and only we, the family, were left in complete ignorance of her existence.

I tried to picture her as I went up the escalator of the Lee Garden Hotel. One thing was certain, if my father had anything to do with it she would no longer be – if indeed she ever were – marked with the accessories of her trade: no scarlet nails or black fishnet stockings. Something in me, a taste for drama perhaps, wanted her to take immaculate and dazzling form at the top of the escalator with a white crêpe-de-Chine scarf and turban by Guy Laroche, incarnating the style of an earlier, more elegant era; and indeed it would trouble me profoundly to find her unattractive or repellent, and therefore unworthy (to my mind) of my father. I knew she'd be tall – my father liked tallness in a woman, above all.

Sina was certainly that, I saw at once as she came into view, noticeably so, and also good-looking and fair-skinned in a Shanghainese way. My glance took in the impassive, unsmiling face and the clear, wide-spaced eyes. She had a subdued and abashed air that might just have been a product of this particular occasion. If so, she was surely to be admired, I thought. She seemed a modest woman, but had for a moment the sufferer's aloofness. Tradition required that I take against her, but an obdurate arbiter in me demanded grounds and evidence.

She'd be trailing widow's weeds, I had predicted. As I made for the coffee shop I fleetingly took in the understated colour – the word 'dove' came to mind – of Sina's skirt and jumper: clues, such as they were, to the unrevealed.

At a rectangular table, I sat on one side and Sina on the other.

The waiter made an appearance seldom more opportunely. We
waited for him to return with our order, tea and a glass of orange
juice, before we got down to business.

'I believe we have matters to discuss,' said I in a matter-of-fact
voice.

I offered a choice of Shanghainese and Cantonese and Sina
said, 'Cantonese.'

What did we talk about? Not about Father, though at one
point I did wonder aloud, in a deliberately off-hand way, if other
women besides her were about to appear out of the blue. Sina,
her head lowered, hardly spoke, and when she did she neither
raised her face nor lifted her eyes. The surface remained
undinted, the shell uncracked.

At last I brought myself to ask, point-blank: 'What would you
like, a regular allowance or a lump-sum settlement?' In fact,
neither was up to me to give, since my father had left the bulk of
his money to Didi, of whom I was a mere emissary.

Sina said, twice, that she'd rather discuss the matter with Didi,
who was shortly expected in Hong Kong. With this, she removed
the need for my next offering, which was, Let us come to ways
and means. Just as she had declined to be the sort of person you
could size up at a glance, so she left me in the dark as to what she
wanted or expected of me.

Very well, so there it would have to be left, until Didi came.

It remained only to offer more tea and, when this was
rejected, to look at one's watch and plead an engagement. We
were over the worst but still the bill could not come quickly
enough for me.

Afterwards, waiting for a taxi, I recalled Sina's mildness of
manner and reflected, She may be just what she looks, *bu lihai*.
Not a tough cookie.

I did know the one about never underestimating your

enemies, but I didn't for a moment think of her as an enemy. Not then: I had yet to reckon with Sina, whom I would not see again for five years.

The events of the next four years came to me at second or third hand, piecemeal, in dribs and drabs of fact and fancy, in the odd long-distance telephone call and by hearsay. It wasn't even as though I watched them unfold from the sidelines, because I closed my mind to it, choosing to behave like an ostrich.

In the mean time, my brother had entered the world of lawyers and so was headed for a great deal of misery.

I sometimes wonder if my taking more of an interest would have made any difference; there is a temptation to think, It did not happen so, but it might have done. Yet I can't say how I could have influenced events. The little of it that I understand I shall relate. What I give is necessarily a one-sided view, a thing of blurs and blanks such as can but be left by a situation in which people speak to each other only through lawyers. The various characters are as I see them, the facts as I connect them, shaped in the mould into which I have poured them. I may not be seeing things quite as they actually were; but then who does?

Shortly after that encounter with Sina, and about a week before my return to England, Didi arrived in Hong Kong to have it explained to him, by the trustee, where he stood financially: the will, the estate, the trust. At the same time, he got a firm of solicitors to draw up, without letting the trustee in on it, a document spelling out the terms under which he would maintain Sina and her child.

So much is clear. What follows, however, is not, or at least not to me and not at the time. At some point in the inconclusive exchanges, Sina broke off negotiations and took the offensive and, the next thing we knew, she was contesting the will.

What went wrong? Was Didi too high-handed? He said not. 'There is now a man,' to describe whom the word 'backer' sprang instantly to mind. Didi all but called it extortion, though it might only have been Sina's way of telling him not to be so sure of her, so confident that she would accept being pensioned off with good grace.

As I've said I only knew the half of it, perhaps not even half; I kept my head in the sand partly because it was easy enough to do so in far-off England, and partly because I have yet to find the distress in any family affair eased by being aired or lessened by discussion. Besides, Didi saw no reason to keep me informed, and indeed it was very nearly the case that whichever way the business of Sina turned out, I would be left no better or no worse off. Also, from start to finish, I never shook off the English feeling that it was somehow not nice to talk about money.

How did it happen that Didi found himself done out of half his legacy by Sina? Only my due, mine and my son's, was what she said, though not in so many words, when she took us to court. He, on the other hand, might suppose that Fate had aligned itself on the side of deceit and calculation, knowing Sina was not what she contended, his father's wedded widow.

The first I heard of the outcome of this particular lawsuit – the first of several – was when my brother's solicitor left a message on my answering machine. For a call made all the way from Hong Kong, it was lengthy. The case, the tape recording said, had come on in due course before Mr Justice So-and-so, whose sympathies, there was every reason to believe, lay with Sina . . . so a good job the dispute was settled at the eleventh hour . . . it was settled under a consent order made by the Supreme Court of Hong Kong . . . what it boiled down to was that Sina was to have half of Didi's money in the estate . . . she was to be treated as if she were my father's lawful wife and surviving widow.

Later I was to say to Niangniang, less from a fellow-feeling for women than from a need to relieve my own feelings, 'Well, she had earned it. Any woman obliged to sleep with a man she doesn't love ought to be paid.'

We were all so sure that Sina was what Niangniang called her, *that* kind of woman. We were all apt to think ourselves knowledgeable on this point, whereas of course we were only prejudiced. Though not intended to teach us any lesson, Sina's triumph was yet increasing our self-knowledge. The truth was, we looked down on her. It was plain that Niangniang, for one, would sooner Sina had received her money in the manner of some poor relation at the door, through enveloped hand-outs changing hands between her and the majordomo. As for myself, I could recognize a repugnance at the thought of Sina presuming to displace my mother, with whom she must – not necessarily but inevitably – stand in rival status. Yet when I heard Niangniang observe that Sina was a mere plaything of a man's leisure, I didn't think her remark should be allowed to pass; and felt bound to counter that if Sina *was* that, then this made her cut of the money all the better deserved. Anyone would think that being my father's plaything was not only unexacting but fun.

What an error, too, to suppose that an appetite would not grow on what it fed on. That Sina (or those who encouraged her) had expanding desires, we were to learn again the hard way. There were some weeks of quiet; then, thunderbolt: she began another round of litigation.

I kept clear of it, and barely kept track. News would come to me, but at heaven knew which points in the series and in what order. Sina was now sniffing out the assets outside the estate, the trust, the stocks held jointly by my father and Didi in Hong Kong and America. Her lawyers left no stone unturned as, filing various motions of 'discovery' of evidence, they probed this account and that. All this took months, a year, another year . . . And English words which had never found their way into Didi's speech before, words like 'affidavit' and 'injunction', began punctuating his Chinese speech like exclamation marks. He was learning something of English law, but he was learning in the dark, having only experts to teach him; there were times when he must have felt that his very existence had been turned over to solicitors and barristers. One lesson he shrank from learning was that it was best to expect injustice, then nothing surprised you.

Each time he needed to go to Hong Kong, to confer with his lawyers, he would silently rage: Am I never to be free of her? Throughout, Sina herself remained a cipher; she was like a submerged iceberg, all the time accreting for my brother's ship to founder on.

The door of the flat opened on a smell of cooking and Niangniang's maid stood aside to let me enter. Didi was standing by the french windows, observing without seeing the night sky above the Tiger Balm Gardens. My pang at seeing the grey in his hair was not a bit less for my having seen it only a few months before.

Certainly takes it out of him, I said to myself. To him I said, as he turned to me full face, but not meeting my eyes, 'Had a good flight?'

'Crowded.'

The maid came up with a glass of hot Dragon Well tea.

'I got your letter.' He'd written to tell me that a date had been fixed for a hearing in the Hong Kong High Court for the end of November. Tomorrow. His counsel might want me as a witness, seeing I was now living in Hong Kong. Niangniang, on hearing the news, had offered a Shanghainese dinner, her way of serving someone in his hour of need.

Didi lit another cigarette as he handed me a bundle of documents. I lifted the first three pages. Why must lawyers always write without commas? Giving up, I said to Didi, 'Why don't you give me a summary?' Even if I had a mind to, I would be hard put to it to follow the legalese.

It emerged (to put matters very simply) that my father had maintained two securities accounts with share brokers in Hong Kong. These were accounts held in the joint names of my father and brother. It was Didi's belief that with the death of one of the two joint holders, all the assets in the accounts would go to the other – himself, in other words. Sina, however, disputed this, contending that the stocks and shares, far from falling outside the distributable estate, formed part of it; and she, named a substantial beneficiary of the estate under the consent order, should receive a proportionately large share of the assets. My brother's contention was that his father had meant him to have it all – as indeed he had, of course.

I asked, 'How much money is at stake?'

'Depends on the share prices.'

'Well, *roughly* how much?'

He hedged; and I saw that Didi was afraid that I would, from an instinct of avarice or calculation in fact absent in me, be tempted to demand a cut of the money if I knew how much there was. I was appalled, and thought with weary anger and desolation, We have not been close enough, Didi and I.

But it was not this which made me lose my temper that evening, but some other, casual, remark he came out with. I did not know how to tell him that his defensiveness, and way of holding all things in abeyance, was merely adding, uselessly, to an already difficult situation.

That we quarrelled, bitterly, was a natural enough conse-
quence of the strain to which the next day's hearing was putting
our nerves, and understood so by Niangniang, who kept out of it
and absorbed herself in piling yellow croaker and Jinhua ham on
to our plates and into our bowls.

The days stretched ahead like walls to be scaled. The lawyers
reckoned six, seven days; in the event it was forty-one.

From the foyer's windows, which are huge and clear, one looks
nine floors down the High Court to Queensway. Light from the
windows pours across the foyer, which opens through thick
double doors into chambers. The doors fall back in place behind
one heavily, but without so much as a click or a thud.

Crossing the foyer from the lift took me seconds, and in that
time it could be seen that a man and a woman were standing by
the windows deep in conversation. Reaching a pair of doors, I
grasped one of the metal handles, and at just that moment the
woman looked up, not staring but looking straight and hard at
my back, sizing up. I caught this in the door's glass panels, which
reflected a bluish grey jacket, an upturned face: Sina's.

Her features had grown broader since I last saw her, her chin
no longer quite defined. She seemed harder, looked older. There
was wear, there. I found that I cared as little to see this as to be
reminded, whenever I look at old photographs of people I've
known in youth, of the yearly thickening, the yearly coarsening,
which has since intervened. Living is warping, I thought; just
look at everybody. We don't simply toughen, we coarsen. There
was something else about Sina which had not struck me before: a
slight physical likeness between her and my mother. This pained
me, and I wondered, as I took a seat next to him in the
courtroom, if Didi ever noticed it; then decided he couldn't have,
hate being even blinder than love.

The courtroom was windowless, churchy in feel and carpeted in a greyish brown. My eyes travelled around it with the curiosity of a sightseer's. Ranged in a row were the barristers in wig and gown, their loins girded, one must take it, for the fray. Behind them the solicitors leaned woollen elbows on tables of blond wood, endlessly taking notes. Paper abounded, pads of paper, box-files of paper, bundles of paper.

To enter that room was to be instantly beset by ennui. I had a sense of coming upon a case that could never end. Would it prove to be something close to Jarndyce and Jarndyce? That evening I took down my copy of *Bleak House* from its shelf and turned to the page where Dickens describes the High Court of Chancery. A place you cannot be sufficiently counselled against, one 'which so exhausts finances, patience, courage, hope; so overthrows the brain and breaks the heart; that there is not an honourable man among its practitioners who would not give – who does not often give – the warning, "Suffer any wrong that can be done you, rather than come here!"'

I regarded counsel for the plaintiff, who was some way into his opening speech and had been clearing his throat a number of times. One thing he did not do was come quickly to the point. He looked like a tall man meant to be heavy, who yet gave the impression of an almost youthful narrowness, with long arms and legs, and slender shoulders off which his gown slid frequently. Whenever my brother's counsel took the floor, this man would make outward resistance by shaking his head at what the other person said and shifting noisily in his chair.

His junior was a young man with a deceptive sweetness about him, who gave me the impression, after some days of the hearing, that he knew more of the case than anyone. Observing with surprise my interest in this individual, I felt the disloyalty of a soldier who conjures to himself the most disarming qualities of those in the opposing lines.

As against this, it was hard to warm to Sina's solicitor, who turned out to be the man I saw standing by the foyer window. In a game I played with myself in the courtroom, in which I saw the dramatis personae in guises of my own invention, this man was easily made over in the image of a slinky, shifty-eyed hood with his coat collar turned up. A difficult customer, I later learned from many quarters, to deal with whom would harden most people, let alone Didi.

I felt my eyes glazing with inattention as the address droned on. I left the courtroom and did not return until it was time for my brother's counsel to take the floor. Didi's defence was in the hands of a barrister who was not yet, but would soon be, a silk. During the recess I was introduced to him and we exchanged a few pleasantries, but he was punctilious, almost aloof, offering no possibility of fraternization or indecorum. I thought, listening to his gentle, unhurried voice, that that was possibly his most attractive feature.

Appearing for the trustee company, which was alleged to have been in cahoots with my brother in robbing Sina of her due, was a man whose face is often to be glimpsed in newspapers and on television. He is at once a silk, a member of Hong Kong's law-making body, and a campaigner for democracy. A man who would not be troubled by any accusation of idealism, he couldn't have incensed Peking more than by talking sense about political reform, the Peking that can scarcely wait till 1997 to make its egregriousness felt in Hong Kong. This man is a star, for whom it might be supposed that any firmament might do; yet it cannot be said that he shone in a courtroom, when set against his brilliance in a populist arena. I've seen him at a political rally, microphone in hand, headband above brow, looking for all the world like a Tiananmen Square demonstrator; and I must say he gives far better value making an appeal or a witticism in Cantonese than when he says, 'May it please your lordship' or 'M'lud.'

Watching him, my mind ranged to all that lay off-stage: Tiananmen, which could overturn a whole system of reasoning; and, not incongruously, Madame, by whom my father was himself dispossessed, and whose ghost hovered over the proceedings, providing a subtext that could shape a story anew.

Surely, I said to the lawyers in a dialogue of my own imagining, you can't leave Madame out of this? The trouble with what's being said in this courtroom is that it leaves out so much. In fact, almost everything. Oh yes, I know what the legal procedure is for, I know it's there to keep us from ever knowing the answer, from ever knowing it all. But must your interpretations bear so little relation to the truth? My father had it in mind to bequeath his all to Didi, not only for immemorial reasons – it was Didi who would step into the dead man's shoes – but because it was my mother's deathbed wish: Together the two of us have sown, you and I; let my son do the reaping. 'Don't leave your affairs unsettled,' my mother had said. '*Remember Madame,*' she had added, as good as foreseeing Sina. He had given her his word; in this, he would not break faith.

He had reported all this to Niangniang, who had subsequently made it known to me. He had smiled, she said, to think that his wife should so much as doubt him: as if he would risk a repetition of history. That there could be no trifling with this kind of thing, after his own experience, was why he brought the trustee company into it.

That history might now be re-enacted horrified my imagination with its irony and predestination.

When it came to my turn in the witness box, so much of this, of what was real to me, was elided in my testimony that it was as if I lied. Under oath, I was false to a truth of my own. Playing to an unintended lead in the cross-examination, I would have gone into the business of Madame had this not been objected to. You are inadmissible, I said to my step-grandmother's shade, when I know and you know that you are the very key to the testator's mind and being. You must bow before facts, facts stripped of their meaning or, indeed, their truth. You, no stranger to litigation yourself, know as well as anyone that all this is played as a game; that it has to be because the stakes in people are too high for it to be anything other than a game with rules that are grasped and abided by. For myself, I deplore the rules not a bit less for my recognition of their necessity.

I spent less and less time in the courtroom, whose proceedings never ceased to be unreal to me. I became bored, frankly; it was that boredom which arises from any matter of which the truth may never be expressed. So much was being gone into, dug up; so much of what had been thought, or not thought; of what had been intended, or not; all pressed into a procrustean procedure devised for the tying-up of tangled human wishes and activities into parcels convenient for the administration of justice, when what was being dealt with was, at bottom, a matter of personal opinion or judgement, no more.

I stayed away when the time came for Didi to go on the witness stand. I had no stomach to see him chewed up in the cross-examination, or even subjected to any verbal roughening. I didn't want to see him deliberately asked the wrong questions so that he would give the wrong answers. I didn't think my brother would be a good witness. To my mind good witnesses come in two kinds: the consummate liar and the patently truthful, and my brother is neither.

What sort of impression he was making on the judge, how

much store was put on his testimony, and, still more, how far it was believed that he and the trustee were 'in league' in some way, there was no knowing. Nor what hold on the judge, with each day, the notion of Sina as victim was gaining. On me, something – an odd intuition – was taking increasing hold: that victims are to be distrusted; they win in the long run.

It had been intended that my brother should only have to stretch out one hand for his birthright and it would be tossed to him like a bouquet. Now he needed two hands to hold on with, and a third to ward off an unexpected claimant. In this court of justice, he was having to give an account of himself, to explain by what reason he thought himself to have sole title to what was being contested. What should he say, other than what would not satisfy: 'It is my patrimony'?

One day, at a recess, I watched him walking ahead to the Mariott Hotel, where he sometimes lunched. His back had the stoop of the tall. Watching that back, I felt, not for the first time, a lunge of compassion: Surely it is sentence enough, to be his father's son? Could he not come to his maturity in any other fashion? All the clichés about sons being overwhelmed by their fathers came into my head. We said very little to each other at lunch: there was too much to speak about, and I was afraid to touch any tender spot.

Following the proceedings day in, day out, he had seemed worried and reassured by turns. Ground gained one day seemed lost the next. With all my heart I wished him well, and wondered in private if Didi made any appeals to the gods or to the dead.

Sina's lawyers were making overtures for an out-of-court settlement, but if anyone had told Didi the suspense need not be endured any longer, that a fight to the last ditch should and could be avoided, by now such advice would have been meaningless to him – as if a preventive vaccine were being

169

proposed for a mortal disease he had already contracted. He would see the battle out.

The hearing was in its fifth week when I opened the *South China Morning Post* and discovered that the judge himself was in trouble, named among the dramatis personae of a sex scandal. One Christopher Harris had got a prostitute, and an undercover policeman posing as a pimp, to procure underage girls for him to rape or to have sex with. That it was all over the papers could reasonably be accounted for by Christopher Harris's position at the time of his indiscretion: he was senior Crown counsel. Uncovered by the police, the matter was hushed up at first, and instead of being charged with a criminal offence and sacked from the Legal Department, Harris was allowed to resign and to slip off into private practice. At the time this happened, the judge was Director of Public Prosecutions and was one of a handful of men who allowed Harris his lapse. He accepted the advice of a distinguished silk of the Hong Kong bar – whose independent opinion had been sought, as was proper – that no crime had been committed and no charges need be laid. Harris was assured that if he left quietly nobody would be the wiser.

Except that scandals have a way of seeping out. The press got wind of it, and awkwardly for the Legal Department – and for the judge – Harris became a figure of immeasurable public interest. Since it required no great insight to see that it was as well to bring the matter out into the open, the case was reopened, and thereafter everything took place much as one would expect. Christopher Harris went on trial. One knew before the week was out that it was all up with him. And the question the public found itself asking not for the first time was: If this is what goes on in the legal system, then where does that leave *us*? – though as legal scandals in Hong Kong went, this one was by no means the most deplorable: one question nobody could ask himself of the affair was how it could possibly have happened in Hong Kong.

The judge's name emerged in the morning papers not unscathed. I had no idea if he had really been irregular or simply presented to appear so, though I had no doubt – since public scandals follow a pattern in which heads have to roll – that his days on the bench were now numbered. (He was indeed taken off the High Court bench a few months later; though, as if to make it up to him, they awarded him an OBE the succeeding summer.) What grief this damage to his professional dignity caused him, what embarrassment, one could only speculate. What it would do to his judgement, one could not even guess at. Against the necessary assumption of a judge's impartiality of attitude, there is the fact that no man is just a pair of scales.

He is a man in his fifties, heavily built, with a pleasant voice and an amiable air. The only thing I had against him was that he did not – as it seems to me a good judge should – set a brisk enough pace in court, and he was insufficiently intolerant of prolixity. He had a kindly smile for everyone, and gave the impression that in this, at least, the outside matched the man within. Yet what goes on behind the bland brow of justice is seldom as one reads it.

The scandal did not lower him in my regard. What it did, though, was to touch me with portent. Some voice told me Didi was done for. I took the scandal for an ill omen, a sign that worse was to come.

I put the phone down, experiencing a weightlessness of the kind that accompanies sensations of physical danger. 'Very bad for your brother,' Didi's solicitor had concluded. Bad? More like disastrous. It was as if, expecting at worst manslaughter, you were found guilty of first-degree murder. You had expected nothing so bald as that; you had not expected to be defeated in so thoroughgoing a manner.

The judgement was everything Sina could have hoped for.

For some time I remained in the same place, the same position. Then I left the office and went home to my apartment. I felt Didi's defeat like a laceration, once I had let it sink in. I didn't linger in my flat – too much was wrong for it to feel like an asylum – but went out again to tire myself with walking. It was as well to have something to do at that hour: I have always hated that time of day, the hiatus between work and dinner. I was then living in Wanchai, not far from the red-light district. The long street stretched ahead, littered and lit, busy with passing trade and lust. Walking, one has only to keep on putting one foot before the other, like this and like this again, and so on until, with luck, one can bring oneself to make one's way home.

Whether my phone call to Didi had made him feel any better is not possible to say. 'Whatever happens,' I had said, unable to exclude a note of urgency in my voice, 'don't let this thing embitter you.'

Of course one can't clear the decks, wipe the slate, and resume life as though nothing had happened; yet I prayed that this defeat would not hang like an albatross around his neck for the rest of his life, nor appear to him to be of his own making, the result of some inadvertence, blind spot or miscalculation for which he will never cease to reproach himself. I have known men whose claim on life is shrivelled by a searing disappointment, whose faces go sullen never to clear again; and I prayed that my brother would not become like them.

The law, my brother had sighed, is rankly unfair. Didn't he know it was that? Yes, he supposed so. Yet isn't the law supposed to be better than the capricious gods?

How could the case have come out the way it did? He

wouldn't call himself fatalistic, yet one side of him has always been without faith in reason or order. Fate had decided this matter over his head. It was probably in his stars – his wife might have been on to something when she said that. It's certainly easier to accept misfortune when you see it as a stroke of Fate.

This has not been a case of man settling with man, but with the die of something cast long before. So much of what happened to his father went to shape what happened to himself. It's like that in many lives. Present and future depend on roots sunk fast in the past. Or is it only that we have simply decided to see it in that light? It occurred to me that perhaps my determination to find parallels in the past was itself a form of distortion, since it did not allow what was distant to grow small. But still I was haunted by the terrible sense that family history could not be prevented from repeating itself.

I walked for what seemed a long time. I crossed two streets, one with tramlines, pursued by the common noises of a city at night. The traffic rumbled by. I watched a couple and their son enter a restaurant, all three stick-like, blank-eyed, and I reflected: So many are the children who from the day of their birth are growing up to be their parents, capitulating to predestining chemistry in the way they look, think or fill out forms. It was with a historical symmetry too perfect for fiction that my father sprang a son on us at his death, exactly as his own father had done.

No sooner was I back at the flat than I dialled Niangniang's number. I told her the news, then said: 'If you speak to Didi can you try to commiserate without being admonitory?'

It was not a good moment to phone her; she was out of sorts. Didi, she said with no hesitation, got what he asked for, engaging in so much litigation.

But who, looking back on his life, can honestly say that he has never asked for something he yet wished not to get? Everything that happens to us, even our death, grows out of our actions and our abstentions, our moments of terror and temerity. Will and fate, motive and circumstance: how much of a man's life they make for him, how much he makes for himself, no one can really say.

After a moment I said, 'It's like a curse coming home.'

Didi had asked, 'What did they do, that this should happen to me?', sensing strongly if obscurely the part which the older generations had in all this.

'Leave the dead be.' Niangniang was angry.

'We can't as long as we have to answer for them.'

She sighed, 'Perhaps it's laid now, the curse. It would not really be laying a curse, would it, if it didn't come home?'

'No.'

There was a pause while I waited; while Niangniang too, perhaps, was waiting. I was about to say something, but before the words could come out I changed my mind and put it from me, letting Jade Peach remain in the air between us.

14

In 1955 my father wrote to Hanze from Malaya: 'You can come now, my business is shaping up. Come as soon as you can. Just send me word and I will remit your fare.' Hanze's wife Anfeng read the letter and in a blind panic tore it up. The letter had missed Hanze by a month; by the time it arrived he was no longer in Shanghai.

It was late on the night of 21 July that the Public Security Bureau came for him: all such arrests are night operations. Anfeng had known that something was up from the way the People's Police had looked in during the weeks preceding the arrest. Those men had materialized and dematerialized, off and on, muttering about not wanting Hanze to go missing. What had Hanze done? Merely registered for work with the job-allocation department, after he had been given to understand that his chances of getting an exit permit were nil. Time had hung very heavily on his hands, and the study sessions he was obliged to attend with others similarly designated – 'Unemployed Worker', it said on his new papers – had done little to relieve his sense of being adrift. He had played the odd game of mah-jong with his relatives, but that had not been for money and could hardly be deemed a sin.

There had been a mass meeting of Unemployed Workers in which those with Historical Problems had been invited to exhume their past for the chastening effect such an exercise would have on their character and conscience. And Hanze had told his life story, with nothing left out. He had not found it necessary to withhold anything, because Historical Problems were things like treason and Kuomintang connections and he could say in all honesty that he was guilty of none.

It being a typical summer night, hot and sticky, Hanze was in his light cotton underpants and slippers when the two uniformed men burst in. Told to dress, he did so. He heard his baby girl cry, her eyes still gummed by sleep, but they didn't give him time to pick her up and hug her before they put handcuffs on him – this manacling he took to be a matter of routine, since to resist arrest or attempt escape seemed quite inconceivable to him. As they led him away, the younger of the two men, who had not spoken a word up to now, turned to Anfeng and said, 'You may deliver his toothbrush, toothpaste and facecloth to the Public Security Bureau tomorrow.' The look she sent him was so bewildered, so distraught, that Hanze, at the door, stood still for a moment and almost said, 'Forgive me.' As though, by assuming responsibility for bringing her to this pass, he could make the whole thing seem more explicable and therefore more endurable. Of the two alternatives – that there is no sense to it, and that there is – the latter is the more bearable.

Had his departure been of a different kind, Anfeng would have followed him to the top of the stairs and waited for him to reach the bottom step before turning off the landing light.

In the lane, where by day everything happens – all the washing, all the exchange of news and secrets – silence followed the echo of the three men's footfalls; the hour was late. Ahead of them, at the opening into Longmen Road, a police van awaited.

Its back door opened and closed; at a grunt from one of the two men, its engine started.

Hanze could see nothing, but as the van gathered speed he sought equanimity by conjuring the route it might be taking. A merciful numbness and detachment was granted him, and he presently mused, We must just be about to bisect the Nanking Road, leaving the Public Gardens behind. Where Black Marias skulk by night, processions with drums, flowers, banners, and young men and women with bright smiles on their faces had surged forward by day. He could sense rather than perceive the vehicle crossing the Soochow Creek. Then, decelerating, the driver was swinging right into Daming Road; and Hanze realized, from his intimate knowledge of the city, that the place he was being taken to was Tilanqiao. He still calls it that, rather than the Number 1 Prison; he calls most places in Shanghai by their old names. For a moment he considered Tilanqiao, not in alarm, more with interest, almost marvel. This was the place where the Kuomintang authorities had housed those who had collaborated with the Japanese, including as it happened the wife of the Chinese Pétain, Wang Jingwei. It consoled Hanze not a bit that a fair number of crypto-communists and fellow-travellers had also preceded the Enemies of the People now being locked up there, though the irony did prompt a moment of wry amusement.

It was when the driver was slowing down near the junction with Chusan Road that, so far as Hanze thought of anybody, he thought of my father. What occurred to Hanze was, He has no inkling of this; he will never find out why he has no news of me. Never.

The police van came to a stop, but only for a few seconds. Gates swung and banged before the engine was switched off. Somebody grasped Hanze roughly by the arm and pushed him through a dark door.

The prison buildings themselves Hanze had seen several times before; the surrounding walls come up only as far as the first floor and the upper storeys can be easily studied from Chusan Road: flat-roofed, grey-walled, with windows each made sightless by what looks from afar like a giant carrot grater, projecting at a fifteen-degree angle from where a window box or parapet might have been positioned, stopping just short of the window's top and blocking the view almost entirely, one would have thought, the prickling of tiny holes allowing one to see, if at all, only in stippled fashion. The windows draw attention to themselves and give the façades the impression of being fortified by black iron cages in grim repetition.

Inside, the place was aswarm with prisoners: it had been a clean sweep. Over the next days, more would arrive, horde after horde.

It was four days before Anfeng had any news. In the interim she could not help doing that useless thing, going to the security police to enquire. Of course they didn't know where he was. 'What is he arrested for?' was another question that burst from her. She hadn't understood that charges could be legally invented.

'Political Criminal', the written indictment said, elaborating just a little. A man came to Anfeng to show her a copy of the judgement, which required her signature as next of kin and also a chop – part of the administrative procedure, all important. The man is tried, chop; a verdict is reached, chop; a sentence is passed, chop; the family is informed, chop. Now there can be no argument: here is the family's signature on the document. In time you'll be able to verify it from the files if occasion should arise. One comes to see the point about having everything written down. In the beginning was the word; and to words, indeed, it would come down in the long run.

Anyone would think, from this dedication to procedure, this assiduous committal of details to paper, that truth and legality and justice really mattered to these people.

The piece of paper handed over was like Hanze's head on a platter. Seven years, he got. Condemned to corrective labour in a nameless place. Had she known that the seven would eventually stretch to twenty-four, she would have howled there and then.

Four more days would elapse before the next visitation; this was the bearer of another piece of paper, a long printed list. Blankets; straw sleeping mat; towels; shoes; socks; and foods such as preserved rutabaga, salted eggs and bread – she was to pack these and the other items on the inventory and take them to Tilanqiao at ten the next morning.

So that was where he was – though not for much longer, she supposed, since from the preparation required of her it looked as though he was embarking on a journey. 'Where?' she asked him the next day, allowed ten minutes in which to take her leave of him. He gave no answer. He didn't know. He only knew that he was leaving the next day, 31 July.

Her heart had lurched, then sickened, at the sight of his shaven skull: the criminal cut. She had her daughter Lili in her arms, then a little over a year old. In another setting, the bright red dress the child had on, her best, would be seen to be celebratory. Here it marked a presumption of finality: like first impressions, the last should equally be deep. Hanze did not look at his wife but at the child, from whom he tried to coax the word 'Papa'. Otherwise he said nothing whatsoever, not even looking up. Even if he weren't taciturn by temperament, he'd be hard put to it to find anything to say to Anfeng, with no more than a few minutes to say it in, and with two guards standing close enough to hear every word.

When the rims of his eyes reddened and he wiped his hand

over them, Anfeng broke down and cried. She couldn't help it; her tears were past restraining. For him to weep was out of character, but now they were all crying, all three. Then a whistle shrilled: time's up. The sound like a piercing pain. Anfeng had never known time to pass so quickly. It seemed only a moment ago that the prisoners were let out into the visiting hall to the sound of the first whistle. Anfeng had been shocked to see how many there were. She didn't know what she had expected; anything but this, this wave after wave of men with expressions like nothing you would ever see – if you were lucky.

When, for the last time, he looked, turned and then was with abrupt completeness gone, her thought was: *Don't die. Don't not come back.*

He was thinking, How will she live? They were living under a system of centralized allocation, in which, as the wife of a convict, stigmatized, she'd be lucky if she received crumbs. Besides, she was altogether uneducated, with no skills beyond the domestic.

As it turned out, Anfeng did manage to fend for herself, although hers was no life one would wish on even one's worst enemies. By and by she found a job making screws for forty *yuan* a month (roughly US$13) in a factory in Pudong. To reach Pudong, which lies on the wrong side of the Huangpu River, and which is about as far as you can go in Shanghai without leaving the borders of the city, Anfeng had to get up at three o'clock in the morning to undertake a two-hour journey by bus and ferry. If she was home by seven, she reckoned she'd got off lightly, but more often she was detained by study sessions and political meetings. At these, she was sometimes, but not always, allowed her plea: 'I have nothing to say on the subject. I am an uneducated woman, I have no political opinion.' Lili was left in a crèche and, if Anfeng was put on a night shift, in a dormitory. Anfeng was permanently exhausted, frequently ill and lath-thin.

Through all this she did what other wives did whose husbands were deported: she waited. No, they knew nothing, the police officers said, month after month, anxious to dispose of her, hoping she'd go away. Her relatives kept saying to her, 'Anfeng, you'll waste away. You mustn't think about it; you must try and think about something else.' What she said, over and over again, was, 'They know more than they're telling.' It was true that it didn't bear thinking about, but it was the not knowing that undid her. These things could hardly be expected to turn out any way except more or less grievously, but it was around the more or the less that her mind continually circled.

When, at long last, a letter did come from her husband, she again did what other wives did: she borrowed money and stood in a queue with a parcel. She had no idea if the blanket she posted – Hanze has always felt the cold – would get into the right hands (it didn't). Their letters to each other were of a falsifying nature: 'All is well, no need to worry.' Their concern was not only that they should not add to each other's troubles, but that, given prying official eyes, nothing should be put in words that could be used against them, then or in years to come.

They had no idea where they might be going, the men deposited at Jiangwan Station that evening. They had been transported to the station in a convoy of trucks, under heavy escort. Somewhere down the length of the platform the destination was perhaps emblazoned, but they were herded straight to a section isolated from the rest, to a line of freight wagons drawn up on its track. It was very quick, the sliding-open and slamming-to of the wagon doors. The People's Liberation Armymen who did the loading were efficient: a great number of people were to be moved over a great distance. The operation had about it something not only military but sacrificial: sheep led to the slaughter.

The men were crushed in, seventy or eighty to a wagon. To enter a wagon was to shrink from the congestion. To take a step, a heel might well trample a cheek or forehead. A crick in the neck or a numbness of limb was merely a minor suffering. From greater bodily discomforts, some fainted, others retched.

All were made fast against the world. Their being on the move belied their confinement – theirs was a travelling prison. Worse than prison bars, these wagon doors, locked and bolted, let in no light or air; but for a small grated porthole, too high up to look out of, these passengers were completely sealed in. For evacuation, there was the lidless latrine bucket against the side of the carriage. Outside, the August heat throbbed. Inside, sweat, breath and stench steamed. It could well, some feared, be a journey of days.

The sound of coupling, a jolt, further clanking; and they were on their way. It was midnight exactly. The darkness was complete. Men dozed, drowsed by the rock of the train, or sat unsleeping. Three or four still could not leave off asking, 'Where are they taking us?' and obsessively considered the possibilities all over again. Hanze, wedged between two stale bodies, looked at the tangled arms and legs about him and wondered about the people they belonged to. What might they be, these dark forms with half-closed eyes and loosened jaws, crumpled this way and that on the floor: murderers, thieves, rapists, robbers, underworld chiefs or, like him, political detainees? Before Shanghai is rid of these, how many more blitzes must there be? *Is* the point to rid Shanghai of them? Or are such exercises carried out for grimly practical reasons, such as the need to populate the empty lands of China's periphery? For the first time he wondered if his own indictment was less a case of his number coming up than a question of his having to make up a number, to fill a quota.

It was during a halt three days into the journey that Hanze got his answer. The halts took place at the main railway junctions, either late at night or just as the sun was rising. By now the passengers knew the routine well, and, at the sound of the bolts being unfastened, one of them would get up from the floor to carry the overflowing latrine bucket to the door and stand there at the ready. The moment the door slid back, another would jump out to take the pail handed down to him; and together the two men would convey it, under armed escort, to a place somewhere in the station yard where it was to be emptied. Nobody else was allowed out by the soldiers keeping guard, but the door would stay open for the duration, to let out the air in the wagon's interior, which by now was foul with the odour of spilt urine and excreta, unwashed clothes and human flesh packed together too long.

This was when fresh air was gulped, necks were rubbed, and legs were straightened and stretched. It was also when clues were picked up, either by stealing a look down the length of the train or, at the risk of a jab from a rifle-butt, by engaging a passer-by in conversation. Voices on platforms would be listened to, on the off-chance that some overheard remark might furnish the longed-for information. Whenever the bucket emptiers returned from their errand and the door closed, the passengers would all crowd around them.

'Seen or heard anything?'

This time, something had been learned. 'Bad news,' one of them began, and paused. 'Very bad.' It was the other who brought out the word: 'Sinkiang.'

Some men exchanged horrified looks. A Muscovite told of his

banishment to Siberia could scarcely have been more deeply shaken. Hanze felt an inward shudder.

'How do you know? Who told you?'

The clue had come from not so much a person as a class of persons, glimpsed in their carriages from a distance, of various ages, of both sexes, but having an official designation in common. *Youmin*, something like vagabonds or vagrants, a rubric for hoodlums, pickpockets, drug addicts, beggars, prostitutes and dance hostesses. The bearers of bad news had kicked around the underworld in their time, and knew a man or a woman of that company when they saw one. Hoodlums recognize hoodlums, as cats do cats and dogs do dogs.

Unlike Hanze and his fellow-passengers, the class of offenders termed Vagabonds were deemed 'free'; they had been plucked not from a prison but a reformatory. This didn't mean they were at liberty to come and go as they pleased; it meant they were being deported not for forced labour as such, nor for voluntary, but for something in between. You might suppose coercion and volition to be all-or-none things. But no, not so; not in People's China at any rate. It had at first been suggested to these people that they might like to become New Men and New Women in the wide open expanses of Sinkiang, turn over a new leaf and, through the dignity of labour and participation in a great national enterprise (nothing less than the Reconstruction of China), gain self-respect and social worth. Had they responded with celerity, had they volunteered, they would have been sent off with the usual gala ceremony, red banners billowing, hand shaking hand to the sound, through to the last glimpse of train or truck in the distance, of banging gongs and cheering. Re-educative labour would have awaited them, true enough, but rewarded labour – unlike convicts condemned to hard labour, they would be paid.

Could anyone in their situation have asked for more? Yet most would have none of it. Just the word Sinkiang was enough to dissuade them.

But did they not realize, these Vagrants, that they were a burden to the state, having to be subsidized or found jobs for (this often comes to the same thing, in the workers' state), and having at the same time to be distracted from wrongdoing? Shanghai was being stretched to bursting point. As against that, there was the yet-to-be tamed wild west and the fact that, somewhere in that pyramid of decision that was the New China, plans and numbers had been arrived at in which the about-to-be re-educated or reformed would have their place: the kilometres of highway to be laid here, the railheads to be connected there, the steelworks and bridges and military fortifications to be erected everywhere and the millions needed to bring all these into being. At someone's bidding, somewhere in those commands travelling down and reports going up would appear deportation orders precise as to time, place and number.

Mop them up, pack them off. Like it or not. Needs topping up? Try laying political charges. Comb the dossiers. Start a campaign. Give us a man, and we'll make a case.

And so it came about, Hanze now realized, that he found himself on the same train as those Vagabonds. Had there not been a shortfall, had the timing been less to his disadvantage, he might – who knows? – have escaped his fate.

'To be on the same train as Vagrants is to be headed for Sinkiang,' one of the bearers of bad news was saying. Unnecessary to add, 'because that's where they're usually sent.' All Shanghai knew, so much talk and rumour had attended the departure of the earlier batches. Just three months before, about a thousand prostitutes undergoing re-education had gone.

'Had a good look at them, then?' The *yeji*. This was asked in a jesting tone by a passenger who, if anything, was feeling less tense now that he knew where he was headed, as one does at the rupturing of a prolonged state of suspense.

'Was hardly the time, was it, with your piss sloshing all over my arm?' Some masculine jokes were then made at these women's expense. This was a case of putting on a bold front, for what lay ahead for these men were existences in which so much as a glance at a woman could be one too many by their keepers' reckoning. Not even during lapses in supervision would there be any coupling behind a rock or a tamarisk copse in Sinkiang. Nor would these convicts come to lament the lack, since desire is sapped, mercifully perhaps, by the extreme weariness produced by hard labour. In the years to come, there would be occasion to work, not so much alongside these women as on the same site as them; their paths wouldn't what you might call cross, and if they did it would only be glancingly. Hanze, though, would get to talk to a couple (we'll call them Meirong and Jinlian) and learn the circumstances leading to their exile in Sinkiang. He is not the sort to precipitate confidences, but something about him tells you he would never report you; and an understanding speaks to you through the stillness of his face.

It seemed that at first there was no lack of zeal on the part of the new government to turn their kind into New Women, their walk of life deemed a lingering from the deplorable pre-revolutionary period. Let us, the Party said, call them sisters, Workers – for they are proletarian, are they not; one of ourselves? Let's set aside the penicillin, even the precious penicillin meant for the wounded of the People's Liberation Army, to treat their syphilis and gonorrhoea and at the same time let's cure them of their addiction to opium. Let them be done for good with that part of their lives which was surely not of their own choosing and for which they must feel shame and regret. Let them get up in front of an audience and tell their tales of past woe – of the parents or husbands who sold them, of the customers who humiliated them, of the brothel owners who exploited them, of the panders who oppressed them, and let them name names so that these people can be brought to book and, if need be, executed. Let them, when they leave the reformatory for good, walk out wearing a big red flower. And let them say, But for the grace of the Party, I'd still be writhing in inferno.

'Only,' Meirong told Hanze, 'it wasn't inferno (one of their favourite words) for all of us, you see. Of course some had had an unspeakable time – flogged by the madams and all that, and made to swallow alum and live tadpoles to end a pregnancy. But there were those of us who thought the New Life – their phrase again – much worse than the old. Of course that was the last thing they wanted to hear, those female cadres at the reformatory, but we'd rub it in. You should have seen us – we'd put on our satins and our pearls, and flaunt our gold rings and bracelets, and we'd say, "Bitter? Wasn't bitter at all. A lotus-eating life compared to this." Pretty childish, I suppose. But it did make your blood boil, the sanctimoniousness of those cadres, the sermonizing, the unadmitted thought at the back of their minds that our lasciviousness – because that's what they secretly accuse us of, for all their talk about our being victims of circumstance – that our lasciviousness mustn't be allowed to pollute the purity of the New China. And am I to embrace road-making or rice-planting just because it has been proved that for some of my kind the old life was cruel?'

She would have the whole lot again and nothing changed. Hanze saw that she possessed some hauteur, as though she were full of the arts these cadres knew nothing of, to make men long for her.

As for Jinlian, she hadn't lived softly like Meirong; more likely, she had cut her teeth pairing off with an underworld boss. She said she ran away from the reformatory four times before she was deported to Sinkiang. 'There were lots of attempted escapes,' she recalled; 'one girl I knew bolted no fewer than eight times. They said our year was the worst – they trawled every year – that ours was the most recalcitrant.' Girls who had missed their way the cadres could understand; but not the likes of Jinlian, who could scarcely wait to return to her trade and fled to do so time and again.

She giggled, 'I was a handful; they called me a ringleader.' From the moment they brought her in she made herself felt. Gangland habits did not drop away at the reformatory door; and the loyal following that she commanded was all but a mob, complete with feuds and fights and tea powwows, to use the trade term. It behoved this band of sisters – a band being what it was – to thwart discipline whenever it threatened. 'The things you think of!' the cadres cried when Jinlian and five of her confederates faked their own suicide, bringing the day to a dramatic stop.

'They said I went out of my way to make trouble for them, but really it was only concerted protest.' The effect of the mutinies in their camp was, on the cadres' side, an increasing gingerliness in their dealings with Jinlian; and, on her side, a growing need to see whether there was anything she could *not* do. One thing they certainly couldn't say of her was, All in a day's work.

'They must have thought deportation just the thing for me.' She laughed again, 'Jiangsu wouldn't have done, Anhui wouldn't have done. Much too near. But Sinkiang – there's no place more remote than that, is there? The end of the world. Dead end.

'They made out it was an honour to come to this hell-hole. As though a high-up had pored over your file and finally written on it: "After careful consideration, your application is hereby approved." In fact, it was enough to be under thirty-five and cured of VD – those were the only qualifications, as far as I could see; though myself, I would add hardiness, if not superhuman physical endurance.

'We signed papers to say we wanted to start life anew – clean slate and all that. Also that we were going of our own free will. This wasn't just window-dressing; it was to make it possible for them to class us as Volunteers and to treat us accordingly.'

To treat you, in other words, a little differently from us convicts, Hanze was thinking.

Foreknowledge of destination was not denied her, as it was Hanze. 'We were briefed by the Sinkiang Reconstruction Corps of the People's Liberation Army, and told on all sides how proud and important that should make us feel. One girl asked me if this was as good as joining the Army – she was almost taken in, poor fool – and I said to her, "You can call it what you like, but one thing it isn't is anything to be pleased about. And don't imagine yourself abed with any soldier, either!" I didn't say it to unsettle; when I thought of Sinkiang I imagined wild men of the hills, smelly and unkempt, with matted hair.'

Was there life after Sinkiang? Hanze never discovered how it went with her or Meirong: he was moved around a good deal, from camp to camp, and the women were not; and in any case convicts weren't supposed to consort with Volunteers. It might have been Jinlian he once saw at work on a ridge in the far distance, tamping down earth for the tractors to roll over. But again, it might not. In all likelihood she set up home with one of the ex-Kuomintang soldiers of the Reconstruction Corps, as so many of her fellow-exiles did – their doing this was one of the things you knew.

This may be the place to say something about the Sinkiang Production-Reconstruction Corps, to give their name in full –

Hanze's keepers, in a manner of speaking. They were constituted as a group two years before Hanze's arrival in Sinkiang, made up – roughly half and half – of units of the People's Liberation Army and Kuomintang troops who surrendered to the communists in 1949 or went over to them shortly before, two hundred thousand men in all. The two armies didn't always work as one, but near enough – with Sinkiang's desolate vacancies and the natives' animosity, they had troubles enough.

Mile after mile, hour after hour. Plains and mountains, town and country slid past the sometimes speeding, sometimes slowing westbound train; but nothing manifested itself to the eyes in the goods wagons, eyes grown unseeing in the perpetual dusk of the interior. How much longer? You knew the ultimate destination but you did not know at which point along the line you should be expecting to get out. If it was to be the end of the line, what was the stop? (It was much to be doubted whether the train would take you all the way.)

It turned out to be Wuwei. Good as it was, joyous even, to feel your feet on solid ground, Wuwei dismayed by proving to be a long way still from Sinkiang. None the less it set the mind at rest as to one matter: at Wuwei those suffocating wagons were left behind for good. Here open-backed lorries awaited in ranks, thirty of them, ringed around with soldiers bearing rifles, a measure of security Hanze couldn't help finding excessive. The offloading was orderly; the loading, equally so. As to the number being loaded, it couldn't, at thirty to a truck, be much less than a thousand. Many times that number, Hanze was to understand later, would follow him and his fellow-deportees into Sinkiang, shifted by train and lorry in relays. Nobody who saw the string of kitchens and barbed-wire enclosures thrown up along the route taken by the motor transport could be left in any doubt as to the

size of this operation, nor the amount of planning and organization that had gone into it.

The trucks travelled west, cross-country, bouncing and
clattering to the thud of clod and gravel. The sun in their eyes,
the men held their hands to their brows, but the scenery they
saw was nothing much: poplars growing out of caked earth,
broken boulders with thorn and scrub, huts the colour of mud,
and now and then the dust-smeared upturned face of a villager
caught in a stare. The dust was thick, settling into hair and face
and palm; and some of the men, feeling their throats clogged,
unchoked themselves by hawking and spitting into the air-rush.
There was just this one road, straight, open, forking neither left
nor right, not even dividing into footpaths. At times it felt like a
road for the travellers of old, a track cut by the wheels of
centuries of caravan carts and the tread of camels. A poor
country, one that would stay wild until the railroad reached it.

The sunlight softened, yellowed, then faded. Hanze was made
to realize they were stopping for the night – again, the men had
been told nothing – by the sight of a fence going all the way
round a large field and the few structures that stood inside it.
Prisoners' pen. Looking in, you saw that here no one did
anything but service deportees. Here no atmosphere of the
caravanserai greeted you, only that greyness and drabness that
armies always impart to the places they occupy. All was
makeshift, impermanent, pared down.

Shown a well, the men stripped for a wash. This was bliss. At
feeding time, the kitchen staff who doled out dumplings (grey,
stone-cold) made their surliness felt by an unyielding refusal to so
much as glance at those with their hands held out. In any kind of
relation with the staff, civility never entered, let alone any
sympathy. And sleep, when it came, was not for everyone the
yearned-for blotting-out of all discomfort: the buildings, it

turned out, were billets for only the staff and the soldiers, and the deportees slept in the open, on bare earth. Throughout the night the guards stood watchfully about, to be appealed to (so complete was captivity) on the occasion of each visit to the pit that passed for a lavatory.

Next day the trucks pressed on. There was everything to delay the journey – the ruts in the road, the roughness of the terrain, the mule-carts to be skirted around and the herds of sheep to be scattered, and, not least, trouble with the much-taxed engines. Each day was a re-run of the one preceding. Not merely the scenery but the stops and starts were of a sameness to merge in the memory. And it was not until the travellers were looking down upon the plains of Jiayuguan that some waymark was felt to have been reached.

Here is the westernmost limit of the Great Wall of China, the line between within and beyond the pale, not just an exit but *the* exit. Guimenguan, earlier generations called it, Demon Gate Pass, having in mind the fact that the chief reason for crossing it was banishment. An exile not of one's choosing: the fate equally of yesterday's disgraced courtiers and today's political criminals.

Who could wish to be on the other side? For a start, there is the Gobi Desert, of which this is also the threshold. The void, that's what we're in for, Hanze thought. Gazing at this ocean of desert from the lorry, he felt the immemorial Chinese terrors which up to now he had known only by hearsay.

On and on. Trailing billows of dust, over low rocky mounds and declivities strewn with gravel and scree, into a colourless horizon while the sun climbed and the heat grew to a burning intensity. Nothing grows in that sterility, save fringes of camel thorn or clumps of tamarisk. Unroofed, the trucks afforded no protection against the searing sun and sand.

Hami was reached not a minute too soon. Had it been known

at any other time, this oasis town would have seemed nothing much, but after days in the Gobi, it could almost be Eden. All is relative in this world. It is a well-watered place, good for grapes and melons; and it was something, after all, to be given a bed to lie on. The deportees were to be here two days. When told this was to be a period of rest, they could hardly believe their ears.

Then it was time to resume their journey. They struck northwest; and at long last found themselves in Urumqi, the capital of Sinkiang Province. The trek was over; now the hard labour would begin.

15

As the plane approached Urumqi, I turned to the man seated on my left and asked, 'Are you a native of Sinkiang?'

'Almost.' He smiled, showing astonishingly good, white teeth, all the more dazzling for the contrast with his sun-darkened skin. 'I've lived there for thirty-eight years.' He had close-cropped hair and deep, fine lines at the corners of his eyes from constant crinkling into the sun.

'You went there in 1953, then?'

'That's right.'

I asked that most predictable of questions: I asked the name of his ancestral province.

Mr Liu was from Hunan, the province of Mao Zedong's birth. Expatriation, I noticed, had robbed his speech of the accent and tonal peculiarities of that region, so that he now spoke as a native of no place in particular, the standardized tongue no Chinese had been born into.

'What took you there?'

'The Army.'

'Was it the Reconstruction Corps?' I asked, unheard; Mr Liu had turned away to speak to the man seated on his other side.

Though the plane must have been flying over it for some time, the Gobi Desert had only now, with dramatic suddenness, come into my view. I was contemplating it when Mr Liu returned his attention to me, breaking in with, 'Sinkiang is not nearly as bad a place as people think it is.' Yet everything seen through the porthole gave the lie to his words: that unabating lunar landscape, fold upon fold, wrinkle after wrinkle, landmarkless, inimical.

'Urumqi, now, is quite a city. You can buy anything you want there.' Though this seemed highly improbable, he assured me that, to the Russians who poured over the border from Soviet Central Asia, Urumqi was a veritable shoppers' paradise from which these bargain-seeking visitors returned rapturous and laden, stocked up on everything from cotton T-shirts to enamel washbasins. He was clearly proud of his adopted city; understandably so, I thought, for it was a place he had more than earned the right to be; it was people like him who had tamed it for others.

If Sinkiang is ill thought of, it is partly because the fear of the lands beyond the pale is deeply rooted in every Chinese, and partly because one is apt not to think well of a place that serves as a penal colony. There are so many Sinkiangs – Mr Liu's, Hanze's, mine, and the Sinkiang in the head of the average tourist. So much depends on how you look at it – as the Chinese answer to the Gulag archipelago; or as the romantic Turkestan of those celebrity travellers who won their European reputations from charting its immense spaces or exploring its sand-smothered cities, or from robbing its sandstone cave-walls of their frescoes and its arched cliff-niches of their carved Buddhas and sculpted cherubs. Sven Hedin, Sir Aurel Stein, Nikolai Prjevalski, Albert von Le Coq, Sir Francis Younghusband, Mildred Cable – these names spell one kind of Sinkiang, not Hanze's. If a loneliness attended these people's wanderings, it was of a quality different from Hanze's.

Although I have travelled widely in China, until now I had resisted travelling in Sinkiang. A few years after my first meeting with Hanze, this place where so few had chosen to come became a favoured tourist destination; at the urging of travel agents the world over, and of books and TV documentaries, novelty seekers of Japanese, American, European nationality came here to pursue the itinerary billed as the Silk Road. I had not wished to be part of that safari. Besides, it took time for all the places I wanted to see in Sinkiang to be declared open to visitors by the Chinese authorities.

There is much to be said for waiting ten years before coming here. Not only has the tourist traffic thinned, but, more to the point, it has taken me all this time to extract Hanze's story from him, this man for whom ten words are a long speech.

The plane's descent to Urumqi Airport was now well on its way. One question more I had to put to Mr Liu, since I wanted to know how Hanze had found the place the first time he saw it that August: 'What was Urumqi like in the 1950s?'

I had read somewhere that the place stank in the summer, from the garbage which its citizens were in the habit of throwing into the streets, and which, covered by snowfalls in the winter, was exposed and left to go putrid as soon as thaw set in. Though the author of this description may have been speaking of an earlier time, Mr Liu confirmed the awfulness of Urumqi when first met. He also described for me the chief means of transportation: *liugengun*, 'six shafts', a carriage 'such as must have been driven in Russia,' he added, 'in the eighteenth century.' The houses, which he said were made of layers of clay and fascines, sounded like exact replicas of the ancient buildings unearthed by archaeologists in the Gobi Desert.

Our flight had been delayed and it was well after ten in the evening when we disembarked. A keeping to Peking time the length and breadth of China makes for the unnatural prolongation of daylight, and the sky was still white and bright to the eye. Stepping on to the tarmac, I instantly felt the heat it threw out. The temperature announced over the tannoy was much higher than my guidebooks had led me to expect, and I had expressed surprise to Mr Liu – we were only one day into June, after all. And he had said, 'It's not usually as hot as this. That's another thing that has changed since I first came here: the weather. It's no longer as extreme as it used to be.' I was quite prepared to believe that the peopling of the vacancies has mitigated the harshness of the climate, as it has much else.

That first winter, the cold was arctic. Hanze would wake up in the mornings to find his bedding frozen stiff. 'Bedding' gives the wrong impression, suggesting as it does the warmth and cosiness of a bed. In fact he slept in the open, in a pit of his own digging. Accounts I have read of Stalin's labour camps in Siberia explicitly mention tents and bunks and barracks, but in China – that much poorer, that much more deficient in building materials – the prisoners simply did without any form of shelter.

The prisoners were transported, the day after their arrival in Urumqi, to the outskirts of Wusu, a town to the west. They were to build a reservoir there. But first they were ordered to dig those pits. With their hands and feet alone, the men broke up and hollowed out the earth; the sides tamped down, the bottom was then lined with alternating layers of clay and fascines, bundles of desert grass, poplar twigs and tamarisk. On top of these Hanze slept at night, with his trousers and jacket serving as mattress and pillow, wrapped in the blanket he had brought with him from Shanghai. Into the mind of more than one convict, there nightly entered uninvited the analogy with the grave. Often, their sleep was of a semi-conscious kind, in which there still lingered the sensation of the body's tormenting ache and coldness.

When winter came, the men were issued with regulation wadded trousers and jackets, black in colour, to mark them off from the free man garbed in blue. These would be caked with ice at the end of the working day. Ice formed also around mouths, eyes and noses, while frostbite gave gangrene to many hands and feet. Just to breathe was to feel a cautery in lung and nostril.

Not even at -30°C were they let off work. Useless to plead that it was hard and painful to breathe – quotas had been set for their labour and norms had to be met. It wasn't until their midday meal was brought, and it was found that the steamed bread was frozen solid, that the overseers relented. Though the overseers were not incapable of humanity, the prisoners knew that they owed their reprieve not so much to compassion as to the realization that it would profit the state nothing if, eating less, they produced less.

The only other thing that brought work to a standstill were the great Gobi blizzards that came sweeping across the vast icy wastes. Not one metre ahead of you could you see when one of these blinding snowstorms blew. The tents that had been pitched for the camp commanders would be torn from their peg fastenings, and if it broke upon you before you had time to run for shelter, it could hurl you to the ground and blast you away. To search for the bodies of those blown away was useless, so swiftly were they gone from view, swallowed up in the drape of darkness and snow. The terror that Hanze felt at this most dreaded of desert phenomena was on a plane of experience different from any other he had known.

One of the most persistent memories those winters left with him is of a night when the moon shone and the wind had fallen, and he emerged from the outhouse to find sky, light, track, landmark, footprints, everything, blotted out by a violent whirl of snow. The soldiers who normally surrounded the camp were gone. He trudged from left to right, curiously robbed of all his powers of orientation. All around was silence, but something drummed in his head – terror, perhaps. It was inconceivable that he should have lost his bearings, but he had, completely. In his mind's eye he can see it now, that ghostly white deadness, that endless tundra, and himself calling and shouting, 'Help! Help!' with every consciousness of futility. For who would hear him in this silence worse than death? Who would see him? Was this the end, then? He cannot now be certain how long he remained in that state of suspense and panic. Before he knew, a glimmer distantly pricked the darkness. It was as small as a glow-worm. He stumbled towards it, as might a desert traveller towards a mirage. By good fortune it proved to be not a hallucination, but a lamplight that presently beckoned him to the cook-shed, and to safety.

He lived, though at times his existence seemed merely a postponement of death, scarcely anything more. Unused to physical labour, and until they grew scabs and calluses, his shoulders and his feet were bubbles of yellowish flesh, pustular. Anyone coming upon the work site would have thought himself a witness to the building of the pyramids, so few were the signs of recent centuries. Hanze's work consisted of carrying earth and gravel from a slope to where a levee was being raised for the reservoir. Here again, one notes the contrast with Stalin's labour camps: while Soviet hard labourers carted their loads in lorries or wheelbarrows, these men bore theirs in the immemorial coolie fashion, in baskets slung from the two ends of a shoulder pole.

The higher the levee grew, the heavier and more back-breaking the loads would seem.

A changeover was ordered every two hours, when the men who did the loading of the baskets took over from the ones who did the carrying. If kind, and if the guard commanders happened not to be looking, the loader would put a little less gravel in your basket, and you tried to do the same for him when your turn came. Of the guard commanders, some kept watch with rifles, others kept count of the number of pole-loads each convict shouldered, recording the day's complement of work on a form. In degree of leniency these men greatly varied, some being merely bossy, subject to a wish to bark orders or to reprove, others being of the kind who believed that certain people might truly be bettered if made to work like slaves or animals, and who took pleasure in bullying the already subdued.

More than tongue-lashings kept the labourers on the hop; there was always the threat of punishment, in the form of the withdrawal of privileges – of corresponding with one's relatives, of buying cigarettes from the camp provisions-shop, and so on.

Punishment was certainly a goad to exertion; but so, for a wonder, was competition. Who'd have thought it would work, this ruse for increasing output – and recognized as such by the men? Yet in tournaments organized by the camp commanders, group raced against group, brigade against brigade, all striving to win the humble trophy – a notebook, a toothmug, a facecloth – that would be bestowed upon the Stakhanovite.

But still the orders were for 'More, more; faster, faster.' Even at his most robust Hanze should not have thought it possible to work at the required pitch ten hours a day, seven days a week; yet this was what he did, suppurating shoulders and all. Daily he struggled to his feet and went on climbing that levee. Unable to summon up the energy even to eat, he would forgo his evening meal and collapse into his pit, thrown down upon that darkness by an engulfing tiredness, as by a toppling wave. At such moments he would have died consenting. The ancient Chinese profound acceptance of the things of life eluded him, and he longed for death. When he admitted this to me many years later, he betrayed signs of embarrassment, ashamed that he should have been so forgetful of his family responsibilities.

I visualized a cool loggia roofed with budding grapevine, the sun tinged a sea green as it filtered through shade, with water tinkling somewhere and a bird singing. Turfan is a green island in a-dun ocean of wastes. I was sitting in the front seat of a Japanese landrover that was taking me away from it. We were travelling southwards and eastwards, in a loop which took in those ancient ruined cities now scarcely distinguishable from the rocks. Their names in Turkic are Yarkhoto and Karakhoja. They testify to a time less dessicated, before the springs and rivers were drunk dry. We were travelling inside the rim of a great bowl, the lowest part of which is the deepest dry depression on the face of the earth, close on a thousand feet below sea level. From Karakhoja, we drove eastward still, until we came to the base of the southern face of the Flaming Mountains, and I saw for myself that denuded, finger-fissured wall of rust-coloured sandstone, which, when struck by sun, looks to the distant eye to glow and ripple, as though licked by tongues of leaping fire. The sun blazed. It burned through the windscreen and pounded down on my face and arms. And for a moment, passing those furrows worn by wind, seeing that sun-baked austerity, getting some idea of a primeval landscape, dry as bone, for a moment I had an overpowering sense of desolation.

I was suffering the scorching discomfort of one who does not perspire easily. Pouring bottled water down my throat, I thought of thirst, of its urgency greater than any other, and of all those unsung men who experienced its torment to tame the wilderness into which my route was dissolving. I thought, as so often on this trip, of Hanze.

The caravan trails had here yielded to a railway line. This connects Turfan to Urumqi and was built, at its most hilly and hazardous section, by the labour gang to which Hanze belonged, it being the general practice to assign the hardest and most life-endangering jobs to corrective labourers.

Here, in this area on the edge of nothingness, tents were pitched, ground was hacked by pickaxes. The hillsides into which the tracks were to cut were steep and treacherous, here at Liaodun, fit only for wild goats and camels. To level them, the convicts dug holes and filled them with explosives. They removed themselves from the site when the charges went off, but none the less more than an expected number of lives were lost, from poisoned fumes or falling boulders. The mounds of rubble loosened by the explosions had then to be shovelled into baskets and borne away, to be emptied into a far-off landfill. It was gruelling, this ceaseless displacement and shifting of tons of soil along paths that never seemed to lead anywhere but uphill. Themselves given a deadline, the overseers set high quotas and issued imperious orders.

And all the while the men thirsted. Their lips cracked, their every pore seemingly sapped of its moisture by the singeing sun, they craved the water that was precisely rationed and thriftily dispensed; every drop had had to be transported to these badlands from places as far away as Turfan and Hami. And to the agony of thirst was added, for men denied water for washing, the torture of being infested by vermin. Any number of bugs and fleas might be caught crawling inside their clothes and bedding rolls.

And as if all this were not harassment enough, there were the sand tornadoes – who knows the desert who has not known these dust devils? Because of these, there always hovered a sense of unknown imminent danger, of ambush. Nothing was more ominous and indeed dangerous than when, with a roar, a cloud of dust whirled, suddenly darkening the sky like a roll of smoke, choking eyes, nose and throat with sand, grit and dried dung. Hanze learned to dive into his pit whenever he sensed a hurricane coming.

The hardship told terribly on Hanze. 'Endurance is something you learn as you go along,' a fellow-deportee had told him earlier on in his exile, and Hanze could only hope that he was right, though all that this man had meant was, there would come a moment of change, a day when whatever was painful now would no longer seem so, when what mattered now would seem unimportant, when only naked existence remained. That hour had not yet arrived, and Hanze still thought of that not-so-distant, almost unbelievable past, when one didn't do anything much, nothing spectacular, and day followed day in an agreeably unremarkable sequence. He longed for that life, though he longed for a life that had grown happier in his recollection. And he wondered if this was how it was, how one got through life, constantly snuggling up to the lingering glow of earlier times, the heat like that of a hand-warmer whose coals are already dead.

The railroad completed, the men asked each other, What next? Of course they were not told till the very last minute, and of course it was dangerous work, the kind that took lives. 'Whatever the project,' Hanze would observe, 'nothing could be more certain than that some of us should die.' They were to mine coal in the country around Turfan; the overseers bade local tribesmen tell them where. These natives, Turkic-speaking Uighurs, had been plucking the ore by means of the most primitive methods for generations. 'Don't imagine what we did to be mining in any sense *you* would understand the term,' Hanze said to me. You might think these miners men of an earlier century, from the way they got at the workings, the native make-do-and-mend improvisations with which they compensated for the scarcity of implements. And so few, indeed so altogether lacking, were the safety measures that the men worked in constant dread of the pit-roof collapsing; and all too frequently it did. More than once Hanze escaped death by inches. Once a fire blazed in the pit, and men died from burns, suffocation, coal-gas poisoning or from being crushed. Every night Hanze went to bed thanking heaven for being still alive. Against these struggles, the fight to keep themselves clean might seem trifling business, yet it preoccupied all but a few of these city-bred individuals. The coal-dust left skins ingrained with grime and turned faces into black masks. They'd have washed with snow, lacking water, were it not sooty from coal-dust.

Cold, thirst, danger, dirt – these were, in time, joined by hunger. They ate all right in the first year; not well, but enough. Steamed bread could be had for the asking, because it was recognized by those who determined rations that, for maximum exertion, these labourers had to be adequately fed. Hanze marvels today that he should have been able to put away so much – more than half a catty (over a pound) of dough at one sitting – and he a small eater compared to his fellows (who needed two catties a day). For a southerner, that is to say, a rice eater, the wheat-based diet took some getting used to; but Hanze soon found himself wolfing down his food without much noticing its taste or texture. Nothing counted save bulk. The meat days were special, but still no week would pass without some pork or beef dish appearing on the table. Hanze acquired a taste for noodles, which like the steamed bread are eaten by northerners in place of rice, and he even learned to make them – you kneaded the flour with water, rolled the lump of dough to a thin sheet of paste, folded it into many layers, and with a chopper cut it into strips which you then plunged into boiling water.

At all events, as far as food was concerned that first year was something of a golden age. Afterwards it went from bad to worse, the quality poorer, the portions more and more meagre, until famine struck and you were lucky if you ate at all. The period between 1958 and 1960 is called the Three Years of Natural Disaster, to suggest that man – or rather Mao – had little to do with it; but with the whole country rushing to conjure steel out of back-yard furnaces in answer to the Chairman's call to overtake Britain in steel production in only fifteen years, and to catapult China from socialism to communism in one short Great Leap Forward, farming could not but have been neglected, so that it needed only inclement weather to make crop failure total, and to face the nation with starvation. Revolutions outgrow the visionary and need the economist, but Mao's stature had soared to a height where no one could say of him, He's not the man for it; where, what's more, suppositions of madness or idiocy would not trouble it.

Miracles of the will were not beyond the labour gang, but the making of usable steel was. The number of trees they felled could have built them some nice beds and bungalows; instead of which the timbers were fed to furnaces that yielded, in Hanze's words, 'neither fish nor fowl, neither ore nor iron'. Yet it wasn't so much fatuity that put an end to the exercise as lassitude. The men were listless and feeble with hunger, and no amount of punishment with blows or words could induce them to exert themselves. To find a little food, to stay alive, this was work enough for the day. Even the harshest guard commanders baulked at making them do more.

How to make ever-lessening supplies of flour go further? You mix it with the roots of wild plants, or you lift off the lid of the steamer before the bread is quite done, and you spray water all over it so that the buns puff up to a great size. The man who thought this up received a special commendation, and a name such as might have graced a newly invented gourmet delicacy was awarded the bread itself: High Output Buns. Hanze helped to weigh each bun before it was issued from the kitchen, to ensure no one received an ounce more than the others, for heaven knows the men were crazed enough with hunger to break heads over the difference. Those who conveyed food from kitchen to table did so in pairs, one to do the carrying, the other to watch for the thieving. Men that hungry would stop at nothing, let alone at stealing, and the doubling of guards prevented neither the stock sheds from being broken into nor the flour sacks from being stolen.

When the supply of greens dwindled to nothing, Hanze dragged himself up hills to forage for wild roots and funguses and any plant not known to be poisonous, but even at its best the desert yielded little, and it was a rare and thrilling moment indeed to come upon that tinge of green which, caught in a fissure or a gap between two rocks, spelled the presence of wild chives. He ate tree leaves too bloated from soaking to do him any good apart from the temporary feeling of fullness they gave to his stomach; but hungry as he was he never fought for melon rinds the way the others did, and he drew the line at rats. Curiously, he was better at withstanding physical privation than those who could have eaten anything.

Above shirts and jackets that hung increasingly loose, faces swelled and eyes popped; below them, bellies ballooned. The men did not themselves realize the extent of their physical deterioration, because in a group where everybody is undernourished you do not remark the empty eyes of any one person, the arcs of rib revealed by thinning flesh, and that strange look which is produced when the skin tightens over the bones and the lips are pulled back against the teeth. You miss those signs which presage death, so that when men in their sleep let their souls depart without so much as a sigh or a gasp, you are always taken aback. Hanze helped to bury the dead, and as he shovelled earth into one grave after another, discovered that he had no more grief than he had strength.

I was told you couldn't get there in one lap. As it turned out, two days, with an overnight stop at Kuitun, was an overestimate: it took my driver thirteen hours to get me to Ili from Urumqi. The road was bumpy, with rough gravelly surfaces and irregular edges, but they were metalled all the way, or nearly all. At intervals we passed houses, a single row of low buildings squatting alone in the emptiness, all of a clay that blended with the earth, and looking as though they were designed to be impermanent. Many appeared half abandoned, or intermittently inhabited. A nomadic yurt here, a Bactrian camel there, gave token to such life as was not enclosed by these houses. To me the appeal of this landscape lay in its scantiness, the relative absence of Man, but I recognized that it could only seem so to urban eyes.

The road climbed, as dusk fell. Dusk was not so much a dimming of the sky as its lightening into a paler blue. Our route began to double left and right. One curve brought us in sight of water; as we rounded it Lake Sayrum broke upon my astonished eye in all its stillness and immensity. Ahead, a movement signalled a line of Kazakhs on camel-back, and I bade the driver stop so that I might (I couldn't help myself) photograph these nomads. They rode along the verge for a little distance, then veered off towards the lake shores. The romantic side of me should like these herdsmen to insist on some ancestral right of way, to claim this landscape as theirs, historically. But breaking the back of Kazakh resistance to the Chinese thrust into the mountains and steppes and desert of Dzungaria, I have read somewhere, was another of the Reconstruction Corps' 'accomplishments'. The Kazakh way of life has been given its notice.

The desert had been left behind, and we were entering alpine country. It was prodigiously green, green on green. The far skyline was a blue-white mountain chain, crowned with year-round snow, enwrapped lower down with spruce forests as thick as fur. The road was threading surely up the slopes of the Tianshan range, the Heavenly Mountains.

An hour more, and it was descending, down to the low slopes of winter grazing; from here wolves still go down to the nomadic encampments to prowl for sheep. The woods opened out, and we were emerging southwards into a cultivated plain and the poplar-shaded avenues of the Ili valley. And the unwilling question I found myself asking over and over again was, Could this road have been pushed to completion, could these Kazakhs have been got the better of, at that moment in China's history, under those prevailing conditions, without the use of state terror?

I had never been here before but this was not an arrival in untracked country. I had been told of these mountains by Hanze, of how winter blanketed them with snow so thick that only the deepest clefts in them showed dark. Winter and summer, he worked on the roads to and from Ili, but speaks least tersely of the National Defence Highway to Zhaosu, built at a time of hostility to the Soviet Union, whose border, more or less unreal to the Kazakhs encamped on either side, feels uncomfortably near to the Chinese in Ili. 'Cut through the Tianshan!' – that was the rallying call; but for a third of the year any road that cut through the Heavenly Mountains would be treacherously snow-bound, so that from November onwards, at around the time the Kazakh nomads moved to their winter pasturage, the prisoners were allowed downhill to labour around the foothills, lest they froze to death on the higher slopes.

It was in Ili, in 1962, that Hanze's seven-year sentence came at last to an end. Because he didn't know there was no question of his returning to Shanghai, he put in for it, only to be greeted with surprised frowns: 'Go home? No end to it if we once let one of you go home.' Indeed the prospect of return would seem more and more chimerical as, year after year, the men in charge told him, not unkindly, 'You'd do better to stay.' For a time he ceased altogether to think about the future, which came to mean no more than the next day, the next week, in effect. When at last he did go home, his daughter wouldn't know him, not because his face was seamed and he had lost all but two of his teeth, but because she was one and a half when he left her, and she was now a young woman of twenty-five.

For part of his time in Ili, Hanze was detailed to work in the cookhouse, not with cooking pots or swill bins, but with ledgers. It wasn't chance that gave this welcome twist to his life, but the fact that the provisioning officer had no head for figures, let alone for accountancy, while the business of budgets and prices and expenditure – so many catties of oil per annum, so many tons of flour for so many *yuan* – spoke to the steward and bookkeeper in Hanze. This officer had a great deal of time for Hanze, whom he found to be trustworthy and signally without guile, and was the more won over when Hanze made short work of straightening his messed-up accounts for him. An onlooker seeing the two bow their heads together in conference would have noticed the expression of trusting bafflement on the face of the one as the other tried to explain the arithmetic.

This genuineness of Hanze's, this goodness, came to be noted.

When yearly or half-yearly prizes were given out, he'd receive, to ripples of sincere clapping, notebook after notebook, stamped with the chop of the Party Committee of the Construction Brigade of the People's Liberation Army, and inscribed with laudatory blurbs such as this one for 1973: 'For showing outstanding application in the grasping of revolution and the increase of production, this notebook is awarded by way of encouragement.'

To be a free man was to be paid a salary, 33 *yuan* a month, increased eventually to 40.85; half of this went on food, and almost half on clothes and shoes, so quickly were these worn out, with him doing the kind of work he did. In those notebooks of his he kept a meticulous record of his income and spending, and at the end of his sixteenth and last year as a non-convict, laid it all out on a clean double page – how much remitted home, how much spent on cigarettes, on postage, on presents . . . down to the last cent. It can make you cry, the grave purpose with which he set it all out.

On my second day in Ili I went up again into the Heavenly Mountains. High up, past the point where the road peters out, beside a brook of rushing snow-melt, I lay on the grass, watching the westering sun strike glints from the water and picturing the spruce-boughs snapping under their weight of snow in winter; and I thought: It is, after all, very beautiful. And I wondered if Hanze ever saw it like this, and if he had ever enjoyed it. And then it came to me that perhaps a man in his position never enjoys these things.

'Did you make friends with anyone, all those years?'

He produced one for me, another returnee to Shanghai. I think they are somewhat thin on the ground, people who made it back to where they came from. Whether this one was a friend, or merely someone he happened to have worked alongside, Hanze didn't make plain to me. He did tell me about the practice of mixing convicts so that in any one group no more than a handful spoke the same dialect. There was a preponderance of people from Sichuan, members of mystical sects and secret societies if they were convicts; and if not, refugees driven by savage hunger from their fertile but overpeopled province seeking to be transplanted to an environment less crowded. With people whose speech you had trouble understanding, you kept words to essentials. This, and the fact that you didn't know which of your fellow labour-gang members were going to be in the next camp with you, militated against the forming of friendships. There was also that odd characteristic of camp life, your knowing people well without knowing much about them: a blank future was balanced by a blank past.

Of Hanze's year, many died of disease, starvation, exposure, exhaustion or accident. One man he knew fairly well took his own life down in Aksu, after suffering one cruelty too many perhaps, Hanze isn't entirely sure. A few escaped, usually only successfully if they happened to be working on a railroad and were able to reach a town without having to cross too many miles of Sinkiang's parched reaches.

Hanze had invited Mr Kang home to meet me and to tell me about himself. How different those two men are, one so broken, the other not. If Mr Kang answered my questions at all, his words were so few and uttered with such deliberation and even difficulty that at first I wondered if he didn't have a speech impediment. Later I wondered if he'd been purposefully, gladly inarticulate for so long now that what had started out as a self-protective ploy had become second nature. For much of the time

211

we just sat there, under that dim light, looking silently at each other. His pale, rheumy eyes, like an old dog's, gazed at me it seemed from far away and as if through glass. They were not sad, really, they were eyes beyond sadness, the eyes of stupefaction.

He was back in Shanghai, yes, that was something; but he had no means of livelihood, barely a roof over his head, and since he never married, no family either (and for a Chinese, I might add, there can be no greater loneliness than that). I learned that he never married because he was only nineteen when he was arrested.

'What were you doing then?'

He was studying.

'What?'

A long silence. Then, to my utter astonishment: 'Music.'

He was studying to be a flautist at the Shanghai Conservatoire. To me, everything about him, his gait, his movements, his hands, his face, suggested that he'd be out of place everywhere except on a building site.

'Do you still play? Do you play now?' I was beginning to repeat myself, always a sign of ill-disguised consternation.

A pause. 'No.'

Another long silence. To break it, I turned to Hanze and asked: 'That man who killed himself in Aksu, what was he?'

'A driver.'

'What was he deported for?'

'For running somebody over in an accident.'

I did not hesitate to ask the same question of Mr Kang, because I knew he wasn't arrested for anything criminal and therefore shameful. He was a political deportee, that much I knew about him. Yet for all my foreknowledge I was unprepared for the answer he gave me. I felt a thump in the stomach when, after a long, long interval, he turned his hitherto unmoved face to me with, for the first time, a look of something on it, sorrow maybe, or disbelief, and said: 'I have no idea why I was deported. I truly haven't.'

16

'And you,' I asked Hanze, not for the first time, 'why did you go to Sinkiang?'

We were wandering down a path on Putuoshan, the island Buddhist sanctuary. We had intended it to be a leisurely afternoon stroll, but we are neither of us saunterers, and from habit we both walked briskly, taking in little of the view. I was here on a writing assignment, and had asked Hanze to accompany me because from Putuoshan it is but a short hop to the Chusan Archipelago, where I had never been; and it would suit me very well if, instead of being plunged in alone among relatives I hardly knew, I were to have him as my guide and companion. There are few people whose company I find more soothing.

Asked about his arrest on previous occasions, Hanze would muffle its drama and mutter something about gambling; but I was certain that there was more to it than that, and some instinct told me that now was the time to ask him again (the difference between the last time and this lay in my father's death).

This time, my question 'What was written on your indictment?' elicited a full answer. 'Treason, with Gambling as a secondary charge.'

'Treason? You?'

'You see, I worked for your grandfather, and my master –' He left unsaid, 'was a collaborator.' And from the master one may infer the servant, may one not? If one knows one's Chinese history one doesn't wonder how such a thing could be, one family member being punished for the wrong done by another.

We walked on down the path, past one of the monasteries with which Putuoshan is studded – 'There is no building not a temple, no man not a monk,' it used to be said of the island. I couldn't afford to give it undivided attention, but the cursory glance I threw the monastery was enough to reveal a carpenter at work on restoring its ceiling, and a craftsman applying gold leaf to a large and ugly carving of a seated Bodhisattva. The tourists, for whom all this was being done, were nowhere in sight and would in any case appear only in driblets if at all. A bird cheeped somewhere, but the sound of the sea came to us more remotely.

I still felt I knew only half the story, and wanted the whole. Turning my gaze back to Hanze, I began: 'If there's one thing communists are good at, it's concocting lies from seeds of truth. Not outright lies, but falsehoods with half-grains of fact. Something that is factual, perhaps, without being true. Also, they like to give an air of legality to their actions, to assure the accused that everything has been done properly, not arbitrarily. So they always have to have something to go on, even if it's very flimsy. They want to appear to have right on their side. As far as my grandfather was concerned, they couldn't have just invented his treason; there must have been some grounds, however insubstantial, for the finding that he collaborated with the Japanese.'

I waited for Hanze to speak. When he merely nodded, I persisted, 'What, in his case, was the half-truth from which the whole was fabricated?'

'Your grandfather was a *lianbao zhang*,' Hanze said.

'A *what?*'

'A *lianbao zhang*,' he repeated, 'the head of a *lianbao*.' He added, 'When Wang Jingwei's government was running the French Concession.'

He did not explain, this man to whom it seldom occurs to speak, but simply assumed that I knew enough history to know what he meant. In fact I wouldn't have known, had I not had to make a study of the Wang Jingwei régime for a project I took on some years previously.

In 1941, Wang Jingwei started what was called a Country Clean-Up Campaign in Shanghai and neighbouring provinces, aimed at squeezing out anti-Japanese guerrillas and sealing in the flow of commodities and produce. To swoop on your enemies, you have to know where they are and to keep track of their movements; the first step is evidently to require household registration, to issue identity cards and to introduce travel passes. For the next step, there was a system to hand: when it comes to social control the Chinese mind turns not unnaturally to the old *baojia* system of mutual security and collective responsibility; Wang's was by no means the first since imperial times to do so. In theory, one hundred households constituted a *jia*, ten *jia* constituted a *bao*. *Bao* combined with *bao* to form a *lianbao*, a 'united *bao*'. As for the idea behind the system, it was to hold all members of a given group culpable for the wrong only one of them did. Each group had its own headman, often a reluctant one; much, often too much, was asked of him, and in any case the difficulty of keeping tabs on people frequently on the move made hay of the system.

Within six months of Pearl Harbor and the Japanese occupation of the foreign settlements in Shanghai, the collaborationist government was ordaining the division of the 747,307 residents of the French Concession into 40,624 households,

4,499 *jia*, 1,038 *bao* and 264 *lianbao*. Leaders were appointed, one of them being my grandfather. With his faultless memory, Hanze tells me that my grandfather was leader of the No. 263 *lianbao*, as well as deputy head of the Pétain District, where he lived. To a man, the appointees were owners of shops or businesses. Some were no doubt collaborators, others were clearly not; all were men of means; none were not under some degree of compulsion. Bad as it was to accept, it would be worse to decline.

Blockades and checkpoints having been set up, it was up to the leader of each community to mount guards and supply men for sentry duty. On paper, all militiamen, anyone aged between twenty-five and thirty-five who was not a physician, civil servant, teacher or journalist, took turns at the posts; in practice, such was the general apathy and resistance that the heads dispatched their own cooks, drivers, domestic servants or, if they were tradespeople, their apprentices and runners. One came quickly to see the point about appointing only businessmen as leaders. The shifts were short, only two hours each, but still the work was scamped, and it was all some could do to stay awake during their turn at the sentry stand.

Nor was that quite all; as district head, my grandfather had also to see to the tedious and time-consuming business of census-taking and household-checking. He reckoned it was a good deal to ask. Luckily for him, he had Hanze, the ever faithful leg-man.

All his life Hanze has been ruled by but one loyalty. It is almost as if he has made it his life's work. For this, he got twenty-four years of forced labour.

'How shall we ever make it up to you?' But as soon as the words were out I realized they were wrong. There was nothing Hanze wanted redressed; the last thing he wanted was for us to have it on our conscience, the fact that his association with our family cost him so dear; that was why he left it till after my father's death to reveal everything. For him to say to his accusers, I was forced to, or, I couldn't not, a man in my lowly position – for him to acquit himself in this way would have been easy enough; yet it was what he could not bring himself to do, since it was tantamount to speaking ill of his master, and to dishonouring his memory. For that matter, he could never say of the turn his life had taken, That's what comes of trying to be honest. He has the perception to know quite well what the world wants, but would not give it to gain himself an advantage.

At my question he remained mum. And all at once I wanted to say, What is it about you, Hanze? All those years, those trials, and your heart never moved from its place? He never broke those unwritten, perhaps to him precious, rules by which relationships and emotions were ordered in the vanished world of his youth, those rules cast in a bronze more enduring than anything inscribed in a book of regulations. I am certain that had my father met him again, he would have found Hanze not one jot changed from the person he saw the last of in 1952 in Hong Kong – respectful yet not servile, stoic yet not resigned, humble yet not self-effacing, above all constant; and he would also have wondered, as I do so often, how Hanze's experience could have left him so unembittered.

There was one more thing to clear up: 'If you had said nothing about any of it in your confession,' I asked, 'would you have got away with it, do you think?'

'For a while maybe, but who knows what might not have been raked up during the Cultural Revolution?' And he told me an extraordinary story, of how, some months into that madness, two men travelled all the way from Shanghai to Sinkiang to question him about our family.

Did he know what had become of them? Of *Er Xiaojie*? *Er Xiaojie*, something like Second Mistress, was a title used of

Niangniang, the younger of two daughters. Hanze's reply to this was that he had heard nothing beyond the rumour that she was in Hong Kong, at a guess working as a dance hostess, the lot of many another hard-up Shanghai refugee. He observed the intense interest of these men in Niangniang, but was not to know that it arose out of her intimacy with Henry, the Kuomintang spy. That they should have got wind of this is as chilling and amazing to me as the fact that one's dossier-worthiness, one's fitness for those secret personal files by which the totalitarian state keeps tabs on everyone, survives one's permanent emigration from China.

Of Nanny Moon? Of Yeshu? Here Hanze was able to be more informative, and his portrayal of Yeshu as somebody life treated unkindly could not but have helped my uncle's cause. At the very least, it would have corroborated any confession Yeshu might have had to write.

Yeshu did, as I've said before, ride out the storm of the Cultural Revolution. But not so the broken images which Hanze and I were now glimpsing. Extensive repairs were in progress, aimed at giving new lives to these symbols of an older day. I foresaw that the corrosions of tourists would trail behind the depredations of Red Guards. Thinking that revolution was a retrogression, not an advance, I recalled something which Graham Greene has written, something he says was perhaps typical of the whole human race: 'violence in favour of an ideal and then the ideal lost and the violence just going on'.

The coast had now come into view, and a tumble of rocks tapering off to a point in the sea. The shore is intermittently rocky here, and at low tide there is a passably good beach for summer bathers. As a boy my father came to this island for his summer holidays. He hated it: Madame was in her Buddhist phase; no food was to be had on the entire island that was not strictly vegetarian, and he had to bribe fishermen to smuggle meat to him. Did he know this? I asked Hanze.

'Yes.' I can tell this man little about my father that he doesn't already know. I expressed regret that he and my father never saw each other again.

'We did speak, just once; that time he called me long-distance. I could hardly believe my ears; his voice was exactly as I remember it.' Hanze had had to be fetched by the woman who guards the one phone in the lane.

Unable to meet the past without pain, my father wanted news of no one in Shanghai; Hanze was the one exception. He sent money regularly, and promised in a letter that as long as he should live Hanze would want for nothing.

'What did you talk about?'

'We asked after each other's health.'

Was that all? 'That was all. But just before he rang off your father said, "If there's anything you want, anything at all . . ." and I said, "No, there's nothing." And it's true, you know. It's more than enough for me, to stand well with him. They all know it in the lane; they all say, "Were he your own brother, Hanze, he couldn't have treated you better." It's because of him, because of your family, that I can hold my head up high before men.' And to my astonishment I saw Hanze's eyes fill with tears before he bowed his head.

Some months after my first trip to Shanghai, Hanze wrote me a letter in which he reported on Niangniang's visit to China. 'I accompanied her first to Soochow,' he wrote, 'and together we went to the cemetery where the late master was buried. We made offerings, though the tomb and coffin were all destroyed during the Cultural Revolution and the bones were nowhere to be found. Your aunt's plan is to return next winter and arrange for the soul to be summoned to Little Panshi, your ancestral home in the Chusan Archipelago, and for a new tomb to be built there and your grandfather to be properly reburied.

'The next day we proceeded to Chusan [the island from which the archipelago takes its name], where your aunt was warmly received by the Office for Overseas Chinese Affairs, and where she made a tour of your old mansion (now a guesthouse). The Office expressly requested that I pass on their compliments to you and also their hope that you, too, will pay Chusan a visit before long.' From something he then said, it was apparent that Niangniang had bragged about me to the Office, making me out to be a scholar – the next best thing, in the present-day Chinese scheme of things, to a self-made billionaire.

That the Office made a fuss of Niangniang was small surprise: she was their fantasy made flesh, the native-daughter-made-good who returns to the impoverished land of her forefathers and pays for its electrification. It was a heady wine, the attention they lavished on her, and she took good deep draughts of it. Afraid that I might think her a sucker, Niangniang never mentioned the electrification to me, and neither, at first, did Hanze, who knows my mind (that's another thing about him, his understanding and discretion). However, she did tell me about the trip to Soochow and her shocked discovery that what had once been the Lingya Cemetery was now farmland, and about a waterlogged patch she stumbled on where bones and skulls lay half-submerged in the slime. Forestalling my question, 'How can you rebury Grandfather when there's not a bone left?', she said, 'We found a scrap of yellow cedar from the coffin in the plot where his tomb was, and that's enough for the soul-summoner to go on.' As to how she knew which plot it was, a niece of Madame's remembered it from the times she had been bidden by her aunt to light incense there.

Niangniang invited to this reburial ceremony as many of her relatives as chose to come. I heard that Yeshu did, from Canton, with all his family, and I could imagine him indulging her, going along with everything she proposed in the knowledge that nothing would abash her, neither the doubt that my grandfather's shade would receive its summons, nor the suggestion that the Taoist priest rustled up for the exercise looked to be a fake.

In the succeeding years, come every Pure Brightness Festival, Hanze would make the journey there from Shanghai to perform rites before my grandfather's new grave. He would write and tell me about it; but from England it had all seemed very far away, extraneous to my existence. What was Chusan or Little Panshi to me, since I had never been there? As for the relatives, they were strangers to me; and to pretend that I had much rapport with people for whom a television set was a new thing under the sun struck me as a tedious affectation. But now I was in the vicinity, and so far as I could be persuaded to visit, this nearness did – I don't know if I'd have gone sooner or later, if only out of curiosity.

The first thing to transfix my attention on entering the port on Chusan was my grandfather's outsize mansion. Rearing four-square out of the waterfront of which it forms almost the entire side, it seems to have been built on a scale of its own. No house can ever have been more unmissably placed. My grandfather must have fancied himself as the district squire. How typical he was – the emigrant who made good and then came back to his home town to put up its biggest building. Just as typically, he never lived in it, and my father knew it better than he. After his expulsion from Zhongshi, the school established by Shanghai's number-one gangster, my father was sent for a number of terms to a school here, and during that time he lived in the mansion, with servants and four Alsatians for company. When war broke out, the Japanese requisitioned the Alsatians to guard the main gates of the city walls, and commandeered the house itself for their own use, as naval headquarters. At war's end, in the course of the victor's takeover of enemy properties, the house fell into the hands of the Kuomintang government, and from those hands it eventually passed into the possession of the People's Government, or more specifically the People's Liberation Army. Why I go into all this, I hope presently to make clear.

Touring the house, I traced the plan, a U with four rooms on each arm of the letter and seven rooms across, the pattern repeated on the upper floor. I knew this to be a Chinese plan, but I also knew that the house was designed by Monsieur Minutti with just enough of a European flavour to suggest modernity. One enters through a door crowned by a semi-circular arch with foliated bas-relief, between fluted Doric columns. There is a sense of Euclidean space, of linear time, that opposes itself to those pangs of transience which haunted the mind of old China.

To be allowed into the building at all, I had had to ask leave of the Navy, whose guesthouse it now is. This was arranged on my behalf by a Mr Wang of the Office for Overseas Chinese Affairs, whose pet project it was to wrest the house from the Navy on behalf of the original owner's progeny. This was an affair of inter-departmental rivalry, and we, as 'the family', were involved only to the extent that the bid for the return of the property was made in our name. 'Wouldn't you,' Mr Wang had said to Niangniang, 'rather see the house turned into a school named after your father?' And into Niangniang's mind there must immediately have leaped a picture of her family name blazoned on a bronze plaque or a stone stele.

In Mr Wang's path, however, there lay an obstacle, to remove which required the political rehabilitation of my grandfather, for it was a rule that restitution of property might not be made to the family of a traitor. Mr Wang didn't in fact know much about my grandfather apart from what Hanze and Niangniang had told him, so it was as well his connections in Shanghai were good enough to gain him access to the Party dossiers. He came away glum-faced from his forays, for the matter turned out to be more complicated than he'd thought.

He did pull it off in the end – by a sort of bureaucratic sleight of hand. He set out the case in such a way that the question of my grandfather's treason needn't come into the picture at all, arguing that, unlike 116 Route Winling, which was confiscated outright from the owner, the mansion in Chusan came to the People's Government via the Kuomintang, who had in turn taken it over from the Japanese, who had improperly annexed it.

One difficulty overcome, there still remained the intransigence of the People's Liberation Army, which simply refused to budge from the building. By my reckoning it was five or six years before a compromise was reached and damages to the tune of 500,000 *yuan* were paid by the Navy – the bulk of which sum went into the erection of a new building, the rest being diverted into the pockets of unnamed individuals. At long last a technical college bearing my grandfather's name came into being, and Niangniang led a delegation of her mah-jong partners to Chusan for the opening.

One good (if that is the correct word) came out of all this: I was provided with an addendum to Hanze's story. Going through the files in Shanghai, Mr Wang had come upon a startling piece of information. Whoever it was he shared this information with didn't keep it under his hat, and by and by it reached my ears. It appears that, far from handing down a judgement of treason, the court which presided over Madame's appeal in fact found in her favour: her husband's dealings with the Japanese did *not* amount to collaboration, 116 Route Winling was *not* enemy property. But the decision was overruled by the municipal Party committee, which would have the house by fair means or foul, never mind what the court said. In any case, the Communist Party has its own way of looking at the law – law is just what *you* break: nothing *I* can break is the law. Hence Mr Wang's difficulty. A Party man himself, he knew to leave well alone.

Speaking of this to Hanze, I said, 'If Grandfather wasn't a collaborator, you couldn't have been one either, could you? Isn't it another case of their having to say, "Sorry about that. It was a mistake, sending you to Sinkiang"? Heaven knows they have to say it often enough: We drove your father (or your husband, or your daughter, as the case may be) to suicide. That was a mistake. Sorry.' But Hanze merely smiled.

Zhaotong, the son of my grandfather's youngest brother, came to Chusan to escort us to Little Panshi, where he has always lived. A man in his sixties, sturdy, with a shock of bristly hair, Zhaotong is something of a ne'er-do-well, the sort to think up schemes that can never come off. Because my father never had much time for him, he was a bit guarded with me, his quiet manner combined, if not with a wariness, at least with a stiffness. I have nothing against him, and quite warmed to him as the day wore on.

His father was a sailor, who was to be heard on occasion, when he was in his cups, reminiscing about his seafaring days and his roisterings in Limehouse. I knew him a little, because he followed my father to Malaya, leaving wife and son behind, and worked there until, feeling his end was near, he came back to Little Panshi to die.

We caught the ferry to Big Panshi, and from there a small motor-boat took us southwards to Little Panshi. Some farmsteads, a few cement structures, worn paths straggling from the fields, patches of dead stubble, a dozen ducks in a pond, a few hens scratching – that was Little Panshi. It is not, today, a land of the hungry, nor does it look medieval; there is simply a skimpiness, a feeling that the larder, while far from bare, can never get any fuller. Is that why the People's Republic of China is the one place in the world where poverty is not picturesque? Many of the villagers scraped a living from the sea; Zhaotong earned a little money salvaging scrap ships; I could feel, without having to touch it, the thinness of the soil. There could be no man, with anything like my grandfather's ambition, for whom escape was not the obvious answer.

We had arrived loaded with provisions, and Zhaotong's daughters set about preparing a meal. The choicest dishes were to be offered to the dead before they were consumed by the living. I hadn't understood that the grave was not in fact on Little Panshi, but on another, uninhabited island. To that island Zhaotong had sneaked one rainy night near the start of the Cultural Revolution, bearing such bones as he could salvage from the family tombs – among them those of my grandmother (the one who swallowed opium). The tombs had been desecrated by the Red Guards, who Zhaotong said were 'no Red Guards but grave robbers who only wanted the coffin timber'. On the deserted island he had dug a hole and buried the bones, all in a heap, mingled.

The boat backed slightly in the water and Hanze helped me out on to a grassy bank. Zhaotong led the way to a clearing below a knoll in whose lee stood four large headstones set into a wall of horizontal granite slabs. I read the names etched on them: my grandfather's, his three brothers', those of their male offspring and descendants. The calligraphy was crude, unformed, cut into the stone by an inept hand. I found it grotesque.

I knew that this was unreasonable of me, and I would have

given anything not to mind – it was no doubt the best that could be done in the circumstances – yet the sight of that rough lettering filled me with an inexpressible sense of desecration and loss. My feelings had nothing to do with aesthetics, but with the absolute certainty that no tomb in the old world, let alone one of these pretensions, could have borne inscriptions with lettering like this. None, however poor the place or the people. The sense of severance from the past was complete, greater than any that could be provoked by broken statues or ruined monasteries. I mourned the loss of not merely some old, old sense of propriety, but of memory itself. And how shall we ever defeat death, if we don't remember?

A little distracted by Zhaotong's thwacks at the forests of waist-high grass that flanked the graves, I went through the motions – clasped incense, made worshipping gestures. My impersonation of a normal Chinese was as good as I could make it. These rites took no more than a few minutes, but in that time another mood, contradictory to the one of just a moment before, overtook me. Everything was reminding me of something else, and I now thought of my grandfather, grandmother, father, mother, brother, of Madame, Jade Peach, Ying, Yeshu and Sina, all these thoughts running into one: that of the past stretching and stretching; of the dead continuing to dictate the actions of the living; of families proceeding to their destiny by walking in the direction of their origins; of a whole chain, generation after generation, vengeance on vengeance, act on act on act, all the weight of what has gone before, unfinished, unhealed, not forgotten or forgiven. Nothing can ever be turned back, undone; no one ever escapes repetition, and those who try are the most trapped of all. The present is only today's version of the past; and there is no one for whom today is not contaminated by yesterday. The past is there; it belongs already to your experience. You carry in you a history you may know little of. Even when you leave home it travels with you. And it is too much. And yet unless I am part of it I am nothing.

I was both appalled and liberated. I stood for a minute longer. So far as I was conscious of making a wish, it was that the sins of the father shall not any longer be visited on the son, that the links in the chain reaction shall by and by forge themselves into a virtuous circle.

For a Chinese ferry, the one which took Hanze and me back from Chusan to the mainland was not overcrowded. The visit had been quite an ordeal, and I was glad not to have a mass of humanity pressing on me; more, I was glad to be back alone in Hanze's company. Yet it's odd how even a bad time over can leave a sense of regret, as if one loses something with every experience.

It was late afternoon, almost sundown, and a cloudburst earlier in the day had cleared the sky. The ferry-boat was painted in a colour that might have been blue. It pushed forward, its bows lifting through the choppy waters.

Hanze was staring at the sea when all of a sudden he offered an observation which made me laugh aloud. 'If this had been colonized by the British,' he said, 'there'd have been bridges across these islands and travelling wouldn't have been so time-consuming.'

'What an imperialist you are, Hanze! Did they teach you nothing, those years of re-education?' I took it he was thinking of the same historical event as I, the capture of Chusan by a British fleet in 1840, at the start of the Opium War, and of the garrison force that was left on the island, together with a missionary to stand in for the Chinese magistrate who had committed suicide. Hanze was quite right too to credit the British with an aptitude for hurling bridges (and railways) across their colonies.

Later on, as the jetty came into view, I looked at his impassive face and wondered if there wasn't some truth in the notion that a particular land imparts a special character to the men it breeds, because at that moment nothing could seem to explain him better than that China lives in his flesh and bones. I can't explain what I mean, because of course there are so many Chinas, which one do I mean? Do I mean the land where people accept their subjection, barely troubling to hate their oppressor because they are unable to raise a hand against him? Where they take lying down what is unendurable to others? Where they so often say, as my mother did on breaking the news to me, over the phone from California, that she had only so many more months to live: 'It's my *ming*,' fate, destiny? I can't quite say. All I know is that Hanze doesn't hate his oppressor because to hate your enemy is to let him do worse to you – in hatred as in love, you grow like the one who absorbs you. If he is conscious of a flow, a current that is stronger than his own will, he thinks of it, in an undefined way, as life. This acceptance of the inexplicability of what happens sustains a sense of destiny and demands a special endurance. It is not the same as surrendering to every tyranny.

We disembarked. I saw that the sun had come out just in time for us to see it set. I told myself, Next time I come, I must look with new eyes, see the place for itself, rather than as a backdrop for my own pursuit. Here was the sea, and the charm which falling light bestows on even the unscenic. And as always in this country I thought, The end of every journey in China is a small triumph.

KODANSHA GLOBE

International in scope, this series offers distinguished books that explore the lives, customs, and mindsets of peoples and cultures around the world.